HAS GLOBALIZATION GONE TOO FAR?

Dani Rodrik

INSTITUTE FOR INTERNATIONAL ECONOMICS
WASHINGTON, DC
MARCH 1997

Dani Rodrik, *Visiting Fellow,* is Rafiq Hariri Professor of International Political Economy at the Kennedy School, Harvard University. He is also a research associate at the National Bureau of Economic Research and a research fellow at the Centre for Economic Policy Research. His research covers international economics, economic development, and political economy.

INSTITUTE FOR INTERNATIONAL ECONOMICS
11 Dupont Circle, NW
Washington, DC 20036-1207
(202) 328-9000 FAX: (202) 328-5432
http://www.iie.com

C. Fred Bergsten, *Director*
Christine F. Lowry, *Director of Publications*

Typesetting and printing by Automated Graphic Systems

Cover design by Michelle Fleitz

Cover photographs:
"On Strike" © Cindy Reiman, 1994, Impact visuals, PNI.
"Have You No Shame" © Donna Binder, 1994, Impact Visuals, PNI.
"Au Boulot" © 1995, Agence France Presse, Worldwide News Agency.

Printed in the United States of America
99   5 4

Library of Congress Cataloging-in-Publication Data

Rodrik, Dani.
Has globalization gone too far? / Dani Rodrik.
p. cm.
Includes bibliographical references and index.
  1. International economic integration.
  2. International economic integration—Social aspects. 3. International economic relations. 4. Foreign trade and employment. 5. Labor market. I. Title.
HF1418.5.R643 1997   96-6545
337.1--dc21   CIP

ISBN 0-88132-241-5 (paper)
ISBN 0-88132-243-1 (cloth)

HAS GLOBALIZATION GONE TOO FAR?

Contents

Preface   vii

Acknowledgments   xi

1 Introduction   1
   Sources of Tension   4
   Globalization: Now and Then   7
   Implications   9

2 Consequences of Trade for Labor Markets and the Employment
   Relationship   11
   Consequences of Trade with Countries Having Abundant
       Unskilled Labor   13
   Consequences of a More Elastic Demand for Workers   16
   Recapitulation   25

3 Tensions between Trade and Domestic Social Arrangements   29
   Laying Out the Issues: The Example of Child Labor   29
   Trade and "Blocked Exchanges"   35
   The New Trade Issues and Demands for "Fair Trade"   36
   Integration and Social Policy in Europe   38
   Maastricht, the French Strikes, and the Social Dimension   41
   Do Differences in National Institutions Have Effects on Trade?   44
   Recapitulation   48

4 Trade and the Demand for Social Insurance   **49**
    Is External Risk Important?   55
    Cross-Country Evidence on Openness, External Risk,
       and Government Activity   57
    Evidence from Panel Data for the OECD Countries   60
    Recapitulation   64

5 Implications   **69**
    Social Disintegration as the Price of
       Economic Integration?   69
    Policy Implications   71
    Concluding Remarks   85

Appendix A   **89**

Appendix B   **96**

References   **97**

Index   **103**

Preface

The publications of the Institute for International Economics have consistently supported economic globalization and continued liberalization of international trade and investment. A number of observers have in fact credited the Institute with providing some of the understanding and policy proposals that have sustained, and even accelerated, the global thrust for open markets.

We at the Institute are thus acutely aware of the criticisms of globalization and liberalization that continue to emerge. Some of these criticisms can be quickly dismissed as old-fashioned protectionism, even if disguised in new clothing, or as simple errors of analysis. But some rest on serious questions about both the principles and practices that underpin the contemporary world economy and must therefore be taken seriously. This study is one of several that the Institute will be releasing in the near future that attempts to provide an objective and thorough reassessment of the case for and against globalization.

Author Dani Rodrik clearly answers the question posed in the title of this book in the negative and rejects protectionist trade policies. He also concludes, however, that globalization can succeed and be sustained only if appropriate domestic policy measures are undertaken to cushion the impact on groups that are adversely affected and, even more important, to equip all sectors of society to take advantage of the benefits of globalization rather than be undermined by it.

We at the Institute suspect that the United States will soon engage in a fundamental debate on the country's trade, and perhaps its overall international economic, policy. The NAFTA legislation triggered such a debate in 1993 despite the modest economic impact and geographic scope of the issue at hand. The next debate could be much more far-reaching because Presidents Bush and Clinton have committed the United States to participate in free trade agreements with all of Latin America (except Cuba) and all of the Asia-Pacific region (including China and Japan), and because continuing negotiations are likely on a global scale in the World Trade Organization as well.

It is therefore essential that the intellectual foundations of the globalization/liberalization strategy, including thoughtful challenges to it, be subjected to honest and comprehensive analysis. Decisions on whether to continue, and especially whether to further accelerate, the strategy must be rooted in a clear understanding of its advantages and disadvantages for important groups within the society as well as for the country as a whole. It is essential to confront the question of the corollary domestic policies that are required to support internationalization by addressing the adverse impact on those who may suffer from it.

When the issue of "managed trade" became a focus of policy debate in the late 1980s and early 1990s, the Institute made a similar effort to produce a balanced and credible analysis that would both inform public understanding and promote sensible governmental decisions. The result was *Who's Bashing Whom? Trade Conflict in High-Technology Industries* by Laura D'Andrea Tyson, which received wide acclaim in both policy and intellectual circles for offering just such an analysis. Tyson, of course, went on to play a major personal role in shaping US economic policy as chair of the Council of Economic Advisers and subsequently as chief economic adviser to the president and director of the National Economic Council.

We hope that this new study by Dani Rodrik will make a useful contribution to the debate on the future course of trade, and broader international economic policy, in both the United States and other countries. Its focus is the tensions generated by globalization rather than its benefits. However, we will shortly be publishing two more contributions that seek to round out the picture: a thorough analysis by William R. Cline of the link between trade expansion and income trends, and a comprehensive appraisal by J. David Richardson of the gains as well as the losses from trade flows. The Institute hopes that this set of publications will help produce a thoughtful foundation for the decisions that lie ahead on a critical set of policy issues.

The Institute for International Economics is a private nonprofit institution for the study and discussion of international economic policy. Its purpose is to analyze important issues in that area and to develop and communicate practical new approaches for dealing with them. The Institute is completely nonpartisan.

The Institute is funded largely by philanthropic foundations. Major institutional grants are now being received from The German Marshall

Fund of the United States, which created the Institute with a generous commitment of funds in 1981, and from The Ford Foundation, the Andrew W. Mellon Foundation, and the C. V. Starr Foundation. A number of other foundations and private corporations also contribute to the highly diversified financial resources of the Institute. About 16 percent of the Institute's resources in our latest fiscal year were provided by contributors outside the United States, including about 7 percent from Japan.

The Board of Directors bears overall responsibility for the Institute and gives general guidance and approval to its research program—including identification of topics that are likely to become important to international economic policymakers over the medium run (generally, one to three years), and which thus should be addressed by the Institute. The Director, working closely with the staff and outside Advisory Committee, is responsible for the development of particular projects and makes the final decision to publish an individual study.

The Institute hopes that its studies and other activities will contribute to building a stronger foundation for international economic policy around the world. We invite readers of these publications to let us know how they think we can best accomplish this objective.

C. FRED BERGSTEN
Director
February 1997

Acknowledgments

I am grateful to C. Fred Bergsten and the Institute for International Economics for providing support for this project. Detailed comments from Fred Bergsten, Jagdish Bhagwati, Avinash Dixit, Robert Lawrence, and Dave Richardson greatly helped my thinking on the subject. I thank them all without implicating them in the views expressed herein.

I also benefited from discussions with or comments from George Borjas, Barry Bosworth, Geoff Carliner, Susan Collins, Jessica Einhorn, Kim Elliott, Ron Findlay, Isaiah Frank, Richard Freeman, Jeffry Frieden, Geoff Garrett, Monty Graham, Steph Haggard, Lenny Hausman, Carla Hills, Jim Hines, Gary Hufbauer, Doug Irwin, Jules Katz, Donald Keesing, Paul Krugman, Frank Levy, Howard Lewis, Rachel McCulloch, Howard Rosen, John Ruggie, Jeffrey Schott, T. N. Srinivasan, Ray Vernon, and Greg Woodhead. I am grateful to Gian Maria Milesi-Ferretti, Roberto Perotti, and Andy Rose for making available some of the data used in this study, Valerie Norville for a great editing job on the manuscript, and Lesly Adkins-Shellie for cheerfully putting up with several computer glitches. Matthew Maguire provided excellent research assistance.

Finally, I thank the International Monetary Fund, where (somewhat incongruously) parts of this book were written, for its hospitality.

It is commonplace to point out that individuals and institutions thanked for their support should not be held responsible for the views expressed in a study. For obvious reasons, this caveat applies particularly strongly in this case.

1

Introduction

Labor strikes in France at the end of 1995, which were aimed at reversing the French government's efforts to bring its budget in line with the Maastricht criteria, threw the country into its worst crisis since 1968. Around the same time in the United States, a prominent Republican was running a vigorous campaign for the presidency on a plank of economic nationalism, promising to erect trade barriers and tougher restrictions on immigration. In the countries of Eastern Europe and in Russia, former communists have won most of the parliamentary elections held since the fall of the Berlin Wall, and communist candidate Gennady Zyuganov garnered 40 percent of the vote in the second round of the Russian presidential election held in July 1996.

These apparently disparate developments have one common element: the international integration of markets for goods, services, and capital is pressuring societies to alter their traditional practices, and in return broad segments of these societies are putting up a fight.[1] The pressures for change are tangible and affect all societies: In Japan, large corporations have started to dismantle the postwar practice of lifetime employment, one of Japan's most distinctive social institutions. In Germany, the federal government has been fighting union opposition to cuts on pension benefits aimed at improving competitiveness and balancing the budget. In South

---

1. See the perceptive column by Thomas L. Friedman (1996). Friedman stresses that the recent salience of such apparently diverse political movements as that of Patrick Buchanan in the United States, Communists in Russia, and the Islamists in Turkey may be due to a common root: a backlash against globalization. I thank Robert Wade for bringing Friedman's piece to my attention.

Korea, trade unions have gone on nationwide strikes to protest new legislation making it easier for firms to lay off workers. Developing countries in Latin America have been competing with each other in opening up to trade, deregulating their economies, and privatizing public enterprises. Ask business executives or government officials why these changes are necessary, and you will hear the same mantra repeatedly: "We need to remain (or become) competitive in a global economy."

The opposition to these changes is no less tangible and sometimes makes for strange bedfellows. Labor unions decrying unfair competition from underage workers overseas and environmentalists are joined by billionaire businessmen Ross Perot and Sir James Goldsmith in railing against the North American Free Trade Agreement (NAFTA) and the World Trade Organization (WTO). In the United States, perhaps the most free-market-oriented of advanced industrial societies, the philosophical foundations of the classical liberal state have come under attack not only from traditional protectionists but also from the new communitarian movement, which emphasizes moral and civic virtue and is inherently suspicious of the expansion of markets (see, e.g., Etzioni 1994; Sandel 1996).[2]

The process that has come to be called "globalization" is exposing a deep fault line between groups who have the skills and mobility to flourish in global markets and those who either don't have these advantages or perceive the expansion of unregulated markets as inimical to social stability and deeply held norms. The result is severe tension between the market and social groups such as workers, pensioners, and environmentalists, with governments stuck in the middle.[3]

This book argues that the most serious challenge for the world economy in the years ahead lies in making globalization compatible with domestic social and political stability—or to put it even more directly, in ensuring that international economic integration does not contribute to domestic social *dis*integration.

Attuned to the anxieties of their voters, politicians in the advanced industrial countries are well aware that all is not well with globalization. The Lyon summit of the Group of Seven, held in June 1996, gave the issue central billing: its communiqué was titled "Making a Success of Globalization for the Benefit of All." The communiqué opened with a

---

2. The cheerleaders on the side of globalization sometimes make for strange bedfellows too. Consider, for example, the philosophy of an organization called the Global Awareness Society International: "Globalization has made possible what was once merely a vision: the people of our world united together under the roof of one Global Village."

3. See also Kapstein (1996) and Vernon (forthcoming). Kapstein argues that a backlash from labor is likely unless policymakers take a more active role in managing their economies. Vernon argues that we might be at the threshold of a global reaction against the pervasive role of multinational enterprises.

discussion of globalization—its challenges as well as its benefits. The leaders recognized that globalization raises difficulties for certain groups, and they wrote:

> In an increasingly interdependent world we must all recognize that we have an interest in spreading the benefits of economic growth as widely as possible and in diminishing the risk either of excluding individuals or groups in our own economies or of excluding certain countries or regions from the benefits of globalization.

But how are these objectives to be met?

An adequate policy response requires an understanding of the sources of the tensions generated by globalization. Without such an understanding, the reactions are likely to be of two kinds. One is of the knee-jerk type, with proposed cures worse than the disease. Such certainly is the case with blanket protectionism à la Patrick Buchanan or the abolition of the WTO à la Sir James Goldsmith. Indeed, much of what passes as analysis (followed by condemnation) of international trade is based on faulty logic and misleading empirics.[4] To paraphrase Paul Samuelson, there is no better proof that the principle of comparative advantage is the only proposition in economics that is at once true *and* nontrivial than the long history of misunderstanding that has attached to the consequences of trade. The problems, while real, are more subtle than the terminology that has come to dominate the debate, such as "low-wage competition," or "leveling the playing field," or "race to the bottom." Consequently, they require nuanced and imaginative solutions.

The other possible response, and the one that perhaps best characterizes the attitude of much of the economics and policy community, is to downplay the problem. Economists' standard approach to globalization is to emphasize the benefits of the free flow of goods, capital, and ideas and to overlook the social tensions that may result.[5] A common view is that the complaints of nongovernmental organizations or labor advocates represent nothing but old protectionist wine in new bottles. Recent research on trade and wages gives strength to this view: the available empirical evidence suggests that trade has played a somewhat minor role in generating the labor-market ills of the advanced industrial countries—that is, in increasing income inequality in the United States and unemployment in Europe.[6]

---

4. Jagdish Bhagwati and Paul Krugman are two economists who have been tireless in exposing common fallacies in discussions on international trade. See in particular Bhagwati (1988) and Krugman (1996).

5. When I mention "economists" here, I am, of course, referring to mainstream economics, as represented by neoclassical economists (of which I count myself as one).

6. Cline (1997) provides an excellent review of the literature. See also Collins (1996).

While I share the idea that much of the opposition to trade is based on faulty premises, I also believe that economists have tended to take an excessively narrow view of the issues. To understand the impact of globalization on domestic social arrangements, we have to go beyond the question of what trade does to the skill premium. And even if we focus more narrowly on labor-market outcomes, there are additional channels, which have not yet come under close empirical scrutiny, through which increased economic integration works to the disadvantage of labor, and particularly of unskilled labor. This book attempts to offer such a broadened perspective. As we shall see, this perspective leads to a less benign outlook than the one economists commonly adopt. One side benefit, therefore, is that it serves to reduce the yawning gap that separates the views of most economists from the gut instincts of many laypeople.

Sources of Tension

I focus on three sources of tension between the global market and social stability and offer a brief overview of them here.

First, reduced barriers to trade and investment accentuate the asymmetry between groups that can cross international borders (either directly or indirectly, say through outsourcing[7]) and those that cannot. In the first category are owners of capital, highly skilled workers, and many professionals, who are free to take their resources where they are most in demand. Unskilled and semiskilled workers and most middle managers belong in the second category. Putting the same point in more technical terms, globalization makes the demand for the services of individuals in the second category *more elastic*—that is, the services of large segments of the working population can be more easily substituted by the services of other people across national boundaries. Globalization therefore fundamentally transforms the employment relationship.

The fact that "workers" can be more easily substituted for each other across national boundaries undermines what many conceive to be a postwar social bargain between workers and employers, under which the former would receive a steady increase in wages and benefits in return for labor peace. This is because increased substitutability results in the following concrete consequences:

- Workers now have to pay a larger share of the cost of improvements in work conditions and benefits (that is, they bear a greater incidence of nonwage costs).

---

7. Outsourcing refers to companies' practice of subcontracting part of the production process—typically the most labor-intensive and least skill-intensive parts—to firms in other countries with lower costs.

- They have to incur greater instability in earnings and hours worked in response to shocks to labor demand or labor productivity (that is, volatility and insecurity increase).

- Their bargaining power erodes, so they receive lower wages and benefits whenever bargaining is an element in setting the terms of employment.

These considerations have received insufficient attention in the recent academic literature on trade and wages, which has focused on the downward shift in demand for unskilled workers rather than the increase in the elasticity of that demand.

Second, globalization engenders conflicts within and between nations over domestic norms and the social institutions that embody them. As the technology for manufactured goods becomes standardized and diffused internationally, nations with very different sets of values, norms, institutions, and collective preferences begin to compete head on in markets for similar goods. And the spread of globalization creates opportunities for trade between countries at very different levels of development.

This is of no consequence under traditional multilateral trade policy of the WTO and the General Agreement on Tariffs and Trade (GATT): the "process" or "technology" through which goods are produced is immaterial, and so are the social institutions of the trading partners. Differences in national practices are treated just like differences in factor endowments or any other determinant of comparative advantage. However, introspection and empirical evidence both reveal that most people attach values to processes as well as outcomes. This is reflected in the norms that shape and constrain the domestic environment in which goods and services are produced—for example, workplace practices, legal rules, and social safety nets.

Trade becomes contentious when it unleashes forces that undermine the norms implicit in domestic practices. Many residents of advanced industrial countries are uncomfortable with the weakening of domestic institutions through the forces of trade, as when, for example, child labor in Honduras displaces workers in South Carolina or when pension benefits are cut in Europe in response to the requirements of the Maastricht treaty. This sense of unease is one way of interpreting the demands for "fair trade." Much of the discussion surrounding the "new" issues in trade policy—that is, labor standards, environment, competition policy, corruption—can be cast in this light of procedural fairness.

We cannot understand what is happening in these new areas until we take individual preferences for processes and the social arrangements that embody them seriously. In particular, by doing so we can start to make sense of people's uneasiness about the consequences of international economic integration and avoid the trap of automatically branding all concerned groups as self-interested protectionists. Indeed, since trade policy almost always has redistributive consequences (among sectors, income groups, and individuals), one cannot produce a principled defense of free trade without confronting the question of the fairness and legitimacy of the practices that generate these consequences. By the same token, one should not expect broad popular support for trade when trade involves exchanges that clash with (and erode) prevailing domestic social arrangements.

Third, globalization has made it exceedingly difficult for governments to provide social insurance—one of their central functions and one that has helped maintain social cohesion and domestic political support for ongoing liberalization throughout the postwar period. In essence, governments have used their fiscal powers to insulate domestic groups from excessive market risks, particularly those having an external origin. In fact, there is a striking correlation between an economy's exposure to foreign trade and the size of its welfare state. It is in the most open countries, such as Sweden, Denmark, and the Netherlands, that spending on income transfers has expanded the most. This is not to say that the government is the sole, or the best, provider of social insurance. The extended family, religious groups, and local communities often play similar roles. My point is that it is a hallmark of the postwar period that governments in the advanced countries have been expected to provide such insurance.

At the present, however, international economic integration is taking place against the background of receding governments and diminished social obligations. The welfare state has been under attack for two decades. Moreover, the increasing mobility of capital has rendered an important segment of the tax base footloose, leaving governments with the unappetizing option of increasing tax rates disproportionately on labor income. Yet the need for social insurance for the vast majority of the population that remains internationally immobile has not diminished. If anything, this need has become greater as a consequence of increased integration. The question therefore is how the tension between globalization and the pressures for socialization of risk can be eased. If the tension is not managed intelligently and creatively, the danger is that the domestic consensus in favor of open markets will ultimately erode to the point where a generalized resurgence of protectionism becomes a serious possibility.

Each of these arguments points to an important weakness in the manner in which advanced societies are handling—or are equipped to handle— the consequences of globalization. Collectively, they point to what is perhaps the greatest risk of all, namely that the cumulative consequence of the tensions mentioned above will be the solidifying of a new set of class divisions—between those who prosper in the globalized economy and those who do not, between those who share its values and those who

**Figure 1.1 Japan, United States, and Western Europe:
merchandise exports as a share of GDP, 1870-1992**

percent (three-year annual averages)

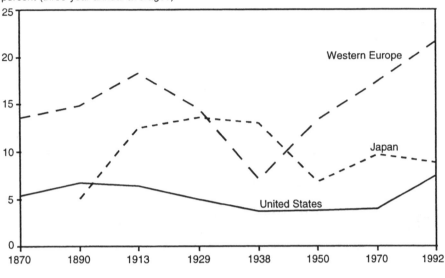

Source: Bairoch and Kozul-Wright (1996).

would rather not, and between those who can diversify away its risks and those who cannot. This is not a pleasing prospect, even for individuals on the winning side of the divide who have little empathy for the other side. Social disintegration is not a spectator sport—those on the sidelines also get splashed with mud from the field. Ultimately, the deepening of social fissures can harm all.

Globalization: Now and Then

This is not the first time we have experienced a truly global market. By many measures, the world economy was possibly even more integrated at the height of the gold standard in the late 19th century than it is now. Figure 1.1 charts the ratio of exports to national income for the United States, Western Europe, and Japan since 1870. In the United States and Europe, trade volumes peaked before World War I and then collapsed during the interwar years. Trade surged again after 1950, but none of the three regions is significantly more open by this measure now than it was under the late gold standard. Japan, in fact, has a lower share of exports in GDP now than it did during the interwar period.

Other measures of global economic integration tell a similar story. As railways and steamships lowered transport costs and Europe moved toward free trade during the late 19th century, a dramatic convergence in commodity prices took place (Williamson 1996). Labor flows were considerably higher then as well, as millions of immigrants made their way from the old world to the new. In the United States, immigration was responsible for 24 percent of the expansion of the labor force during the 40 years before World War I (Williamson 1996, appendix table 1). As for capital mobility, the share of net capital outflows in GNP was much higher in the United Kingdom during the classical gold standard than it has been since.

Does this earlier period of globalization hold any lessons for our current situation? It well might. There is some evidence, for example, that trade and migration had significant consequences for income distribution. According to Jeffrey Williamson, "[G]lobalization . . . accounted for more than half of the rising inequality in rich, labor-scarce countries [e.g., the United States, Argentina, and Australia] and for a little more than a quarter of the falling inequality in poor, labor-abundant countries [e.g., Sweden, Denmark, and Ireland]" in the period before World War I (1996, 19). Equally to the point are the political consequences of these changes:

> There is a literature almost a century old that argues that immigration hurt American labor and accounted for much of the rise in inequality from the 1890s to World War I, so much so that a labor-sympathetic Congress passed immigration quotas. There is a literature even older that argues that a New World grain invasion eroded land rents in Europe, so much so that landowner-dominated Continental Parliaments raised tariffs to help protect them from the impact of globalization. (Williamson 1996, 1)

Williamson (1996, 20) concludes that "the inequality trends which globalization produced are at least partly responsible for the interwar retreat from globalization [which appeared] first in the rich industrial trading partners."

Moreover, there are some key differences that make today's global economy more contentious. First, restrictions on immigration were not as common during the 19th century, and consequently labor's international mobility was more comparable to that of capital. Consequently, the asymmetry between mobile capital (physical and human) and immobile "natural" labor, which characterizes the present situation, is a relatively recent phenomenon. Second, there was little head-on international competition in identical or similar products during the previous century, and most trade consisted of the exchange of noncompeting products, such as primary products for manufactured goods. The aggregate trade ratios do not reflect the "vast increase in the exposure of tradable goods industries to international competition" that is now taking place compared with the situation in the 1890s (Irwin 1996, 42). Third, and perhaps most important, governments had not yet been called on to perform social-welfare functions on a large scale, such as ensuring adequate levels of employment, establishing social safety nets, providing medical and social insurance, and caring for the poor. This shift in the perceived role of government is also a relatively recent transformation, one that makes life in an interdependent economy considerably more difficult for today's policymakers.

At any rate, the lesson from history seems to be that continued globalization cannot be taken for granted. If its consequences are not managed wisely and creatively, a retreat from openness becomes a distinct possibility.

Implications

So has international economic integration gone too far? Not if policymakers act wisely and imaginatively.

We need to be upfront about the irreversibility of the many changes that have occurred in the global economy. Advances in communications and transportation mean that large segments of national economies are much more exposed to international trade and capital flows than they have ever been, regardless of what policymakers choose to do. There is only limited scope for government policy to make a difference. In addition, a serious retreat into protectionism would hurt the many groups that benefit from trade and would result in the same kind of social conflicts that globalization itself generates. We have to recognize that erecting trade barriers will help in only a limited set of circumstances and that trade policies will rarely be the best response to the problems that will be discussed here. Transfer and social insurance programs will generally dominate. In short, the genie cannot be stuffed back into the bottle, even if it were desirable to do so. We will need more imaginative and more subtle responses. I will suggest some guidelines in the concluding chapter.

Even so, my primary purpose in this book is not prescriptive; it is to broaden the debate on the consequences of globalization by probing deeper into some of the dimensions that have received insufficient attention and ultimately recasting the debate so as to facilitate a more productive dialogue between opposing groups and interests. It is only through greater understanding of what is at stake that we can hope to develop appropriate public policies.

One final introductory note. I hope the reader will soon realize that this book is not a one-sided brief *against* globalization. Indeed, the major benefit of clarifying and adding rigor to some of the arguments against trade is that it helps us draw a distinction between objections that are valid (or at least logically coherent) and objections that aren't. From this perspective, what I end up doing, at least on occasion, is strengthening the arsenal of arguments in favor of free trade. If this book is viewed as controversial, it will have done its job; I have failed if it is perceived as polemical.

The chapters that follow will elaborate on the three sources of tension between globalization and society identified above and will review the relevant empirical evidence. The objectives will be to cast the debate in terms that both sides—economists and populists alike—can join, marshal evidence on the likely significance of the tension in question, and where there is evidence for serious concern, open the debate on possible remedies.

economists

+ populists

2

Consequences of Trade for Labor Markets and the Employment Relationship

Since the second half of the 1970s, US and Western European labor markets have been performing very badly as far as lower-skilled groups are concerned. As a distinguished labor economist puts it, "An economic disaster has befallen low skill Americans" (Freeman 1996a, 2).

The disaster has two reinforcing ingredients. One is the widening wage premium for skill, which finds expression in an erosion of the real earnings of high school dropouts: the real hourly wages of young males with 12 or fewer years of schooling has dropped by more than 20 percent in the last two decades. The second ingredient is a significant increase in labor-market instability and insecurity, finding expression in greater short-term volatility in earnings and hours worked and an increase in inequality *within* skill groups. Low-skilled workers bear the brunt of this instability. Rates of job loss are up as well, but apparently the increase is less concentrated at the bottom end of the earnings distribution. The anxiety and insecurity these trends generate are reflected in opinion polls.[1] In continental Europe, meanwhile, real wages at the bottom of the skill distribution have risen, but at the cost of a significant increase in unemployment, especially relative to the United States (Freeman 1996a). In short, neither the United States nor Europe has been able to generate a steady growth of "good jobs."

---

1. Levy (1996) reviews some recent polls and finds that respondents are typically more positive about their personal situations than about the economy at large. He also finds considerable nervousness and pessimism about the future.

The troubled state of labor markets in advanced industrial economies has led many influential groups in society—policymakers, labor advocates, and pundits in general—to link these ills directly to globalization. These groups have alleged that intensified competition from low-wage countries, both as sources of imports and as hosts for foreign investors, is largely responsible for the deteriorating fortunes of low-skilled workers. On the other hand, most trade economists have argued that while trade with low-wage countries may have contributed to the trends described above, such trade is still too small to have had a significant effect on labor-market outcomes in the North. These economists have preferred to put the lion's share of the blame on skill-biased technological change, which is alleged to have reduced the demand for low-skilled workers.

Ironically, in absolving trade from any significant responsibility for the malaise in industrial-country labor markets, economists have taken a tack that sits uncomfortably with their faith in the benefits of free trade. A cornerstone of traditional trade theory is that trade with labor-abundant countries reduces real wages in rich countries—or increases unemployment if wages are artificially fixed. Indeed, in the standard factor-endowments model, trade creates gains for nations precisely by altering the relative domestic scarcity of factors of production such as labor. Hence, saying that the impact of globalization on advanced-country labor markets is quantitatively rather small in the real world and is overshadowed by other phenomena (such as technological change) is no different from saying that the gains from trade have in practice been small. Conversely, if one believes that expanded trade has been a source of many of the good things that advanced industrial economies have experienced in the last few decades, one is forced to presume that trade has also had many of the negative consequences that its opponents have alleged.

This chapter focuses on two channels through which globalization affects labor markets in the North. The first of these, and the one that has been most extensively examined in the literature, is the effect on the relative demands for skilled and unskilled workers. Since the developing countries tend to export goods that make relatively intensive use of low-skilled labor, trade with these countries displaces low-skilled, labor-intensive production in the United States and Western Europe and thereby reduces the demand for low-skilled labor there. In technical terms, trade results in an *inward shift* in the demand curve for low-skilled labor in these advanced countries.

The second channel has to do with the greater ease with which domestic workers, particularly of the low-skills type, can be substituted by other workers across national borders, either through trade (outsourcing) or through foreign direct investment (FDI). Using technical terms again, trade *flattens* the demand curve for labor at home and increases the elasticity of demand for labor—that is, trade increases the degree to which employers can react to changes in prevailing wages by outsourcing or investing abroad. Taken together, an inward shift and a flattening of the demand curves for low-skilled workers reduce average earnings for low-skilled workers while increasing both the dispersion of earnings among such workers and the volatility in wages and hours worked. This can explain why life has become more precarious, and insecurity greater, for vast segments of the working population.

Consequences of Trade with Countries Having Abundant Unskilled Labor

Among the many possible effects that globalization can have on labor markets, the relationship between trade with developing countries and the rise in the skill premium has been the subject of economists' most extensive scrutiny (among the leading studies are Borjas, Freeman, and Katz 1992; Lawrence and Slaughter 1993; Wood 1994; Sachs and Shatz 1994; Leamer 1996). There are also a number of useful surveys and evaluations of the literature (Wood 1995; Richardson 1995; Freeman 1996a; Cline 1997).

The reason that this question has received so much attention is that there are solid theoretical reasons to believe that increased exposure to trade with low-income countries will widen the skill premium in the advanced countries. This implication follows rather directly from the reigning theory of international trade: the Heckscher-Ohlin-Samuelson factor endowments model. Consider a country that is well endowed in skilled workers, such as the United States. Suppose that it suddenly becomes possible for this country to trade with another country that is well endowed with unskilled labor, say China, because, for example, China liberalizes its trade regime and hence becomes an active participant in international trade. Naturally, China will export low-skill-intensive products to the US market and import high-skill-intensive goods in return. According to the theory, as long as Chinese exports replace some domestic production in the United States, this will result in a fall in the relative demand for unskilled workers in the United States compared with the demand for skilled workers. This, in turn, will increase the skill premium in the United States (and reduce it in China). Every student of trade theory has been taught some version of this basic story.

Hence the empirical studies have focused on the question, how much has trade reduced the demand for unskilled labor in the developed countries? The conclusion has generally been "some but not a whole lot." As Krugman (1995, 2-3) puts it:

> It is probably fair to say ... that the majority view among serious economic analysts is that international trade has had only a limited impact on wages. Skepticism about the effects of trade on wages rests essentially on the observation

that despite its growth, trade is still quite small compared with the economies of advanced nations. In particular, imports of manufactured goods from developing countries are still only about 2 percent of the combined GDP of the OECD. The conventional wisdom is that trade flows of this limited magnitude cannot explain the very large changes in relative factor prices that have occurred—in particular, the roughly 30 percent rise in the wage premium associated with a college education that has taken place in the United States since the 1970s.

So one reason the empirical models yield meager effects is that the relevant flows of trade are small. Note that Krugman's 2 percent figure refers to trade with developing countries alone. The reason that this is the relevant number in this context is that, according to the Heckscher-Ohlin model, only trade with countries that differ in their relative factor endowments (e.g., unskilled labor versus skilled labor) should matter for relative wages. So the bulk of trade, which takes place *among* industrial countries with similar factor endowments, is assumed to have no effect on labor markets and therefore does not enter the empirical analysis in any meaningful manner. As I will elaborate below, this assumption is one important reason the existing methodologies have underestimated the effect of trade on labor markets.

Even within the confines of this narrow approach, however, one can generate much greater estimates by considering the role of immigration from low-skill countries, along with trade. Borjas, Freeman, and Katz (1992) do this for the United States by calculating the factor content of trade and immigration flows together. Using reasonable estimates of the elasticity of substitution between skilled and unskilled workers, they conclude that about 40 percent of the increased wage differential between high school dropouts and other workers can be attributed to these two forces at work.

A second reason that many trade economists have discounted the effect of trade—along with results such as those of Borjas, Freeman, and Katz (1992)—is that the mechanism outlined above must operate through product prices. In the canonical factor endowments model, the skill premium can rise *only* if there is a corresponding fall in the relative price of low-skill-intensive goods. Since it has been difficult to document significant changes in this relative price for the decade of the 1980s, during which most of the wage effects took place, the conclusion has been that neither trade nor immigration could have played a significant role (Bhagwati 1991; Lawrence and Slaughter 1993).

By going outside the Heckscher-Ohlin theory, one can generate additional channels through which trade with developing countries widens the skill premium. Wood (1994), for example, argues for a much larger role for trade on the basis of two key assumptions. One is that import competition has driven out of operation many of the most low-skill-intensive activities that would otherwise have been active in the advanced countries. Calculations of the implied factor content of trade that look at *existing* factor proportions in the remaining import-competing activities therefore underestimate the reduction in the demand for unskilled workers as a consequence of trade. Second, he assumes that import competition from the South has induced labor-saving technological change in the North. At least some of the technological changes to which many trade economists have attributed the rising skill premium could be caused by trade itself.

Borjas and Ramey (1995) focus on labor's share in the rents in certain imperfectly competitive industries (i.e., those that enjoy market power). In their story, import penetration in durable goods industries, unaccompanied by increased exports, results in a higher skill premium:

> [M]ost of the workers in durable goods manufacturing are high school dropouts or high school graduates. These workers tend to share the rents in their industry in the form of wage premiums; workers in industries with larger rents earn a higher premium. When foreign firms enter markets (domestic or foreign) in which domestic firms have substantial market power, they capture rents that would otherwise go to the domestic industry. This entry increases the relative wage of college graduates in two ways. First, because the rents of domestic firms have fallen, the wage premium of workers remaining in those industries decreases. Second, to the extent that foreign competition reduces employment in the concentrated industries, many of the workers must move to the lower paying competitive sectors of the economy. Overall, the wage of less educated workers falls relative to that of college graduates. (1080)

Borjas and Ramey suggest that the decline in employment in such industries may account for up to 23 percent of the change in wage inequality (1995, 1078). This conclusion has been disputed by Lawrence (1996, chapter 4), who argues that there is no evidence of a decline in the wage differential between high-wage and low-wage sectors and that trade may actually have pushed workers into the high-rent sectors (which in the United States tend to be exportables).

The twists and turns of this debate have been well chronicled by Cline (1997), who surveys and critically evaluates these and other empirical studies. Since I have little new to contribute to this particular debate, I am content to take Cline's own conclusion: "My own point estimate is that international influences contributed about 20 percent of the rising wage inequality in the 1980s" (177). As he notes, this is at the upper end of the 10 to 20 percent range that most trade economists would be happy with.

Regardless of whether one takes 10 or 20 percent as the more realistic number, however, a few points of elaboration are in order. As I have already argued, this number has been generated by taking a very narrow cut at the issues, a point that will be amplified in the next section. Second, in some sense neither 10 nor 20 is really a small number. Economics is notoriously bad at quantifying forces that most people believe are quite important. For example, no widely accepted model attributes to postwar trade liberalization more than a very tiny fraction of the increased prosperity of the advanced industrial countries. Yet most economists do believe that expanding trade was very important in this progress.

The empirical evidence for what is the leading contender for an alternative cause of rising wage inequality—skill-biased technological change—is far from overwhelming.[2] Note, moreover, that it is difficult to treat technological change as being entirely *independent* from trade. Trade may act as a conduit for technology and create pressures for technological change. When Rupert Murdoch goes on a global buying spree and replaces workers with machines at all the newspapers he acquires, it is not at all clear that the resulting labor-market pressures should be attributed to technological change rather than globalization.[3] Hence, when economists say that the effect of trade is "small," they are certainly not saying that it is small relative to some other cause that they have actually identified. Statements of the sort "trade has been of secondary importance compared with technical change" are therefore inaccurate.

Consequences of a More Elastic Demand for Workers

In an economy that is more open to foreign trade and investment, the demand for labor will generally be more responsive to changes in the price of labor, or more elastic. The reason is that employers and the final consumers can substitute foreign workers for domestic workers more easily—either by investing abroad or by importing the products made by foreign workers. Since the demand for labor is a *derived* demand, which varies proportionately with the elasticity of demand for goods, the integration of goods markets alone makes the demand for domestic labor more elastic (Richardson and Khripounova 1996). The point is put graphically by labor representative Thomas R. Donahue (quoted in US Department of Labor 1994, 47):

> [T]he world has become a huge bazaar with nations peddling their work forces in competition against one another, offering the lowest prices for doing business. The customers, of course, are the multinational corporations.

In the standard Heckscher-Ohlin trade model, domestic labor demand is in fact perfectly elastic (infinitely responsive to changes in wage costs) as long as there is incomplete specialization, even in the absence of foreign

---

2. Perhaps the most convincing paper on this score is Berman, Machin, and Bound (1996).

3. The Murdoch example was given by Eli Berman during his presentation of the Berman, Machin, and Bound (1996) paper at the 1996 Summer Institute of the National Bureau of Economic Research, Cambridge, MA.

investment.[4] More generally, the demand for any factor of production (such as labor) becomes more elastic when other factors (such as capital) can respond to changes in the economic environment with greater ease (by moving offshore, for example).[5]

One of the most robust findings in the empirical literature on trade is that trade integration increases the elasticity of demand for goods faced by domestic producers, a fact revealed by a reduction in price-cost margins. Since, as mentioned above, the demand for labor is a derived demand with a direct link between the elasticities of demand in product and labor markets, this evidence has an obvious bearing here. In a recent study, Matthew Slaughter has provided even more telling evidence. Slaughter (1996) documents that the demand for production labor in the United States has become more elastic since the 1960s in most two-digit manufacturing industries and that the labor demand elasticity tends to be higher (in absolute value) in industries that exhibit greater levels of international integration. Similarly, Richardson and Khripounova (1996) report a doubling of the cross-sectional elasticity of demand between 1979 and 1991 for production workers but (interestingly) not for nonproduction workers. Note that the relevant measures of openness in this context are not the volumes of trade or investment, but the *ease* with which international transactions can be carried out.

While much of this is well recognized, the implications on the workings of the labor market have not received much attention. As noted above, the economics literature has focused on identifying how far the demand curve for low-skilled labor has shifted down and not on the consequences of the increase in the elasticity of this demand. Focusing on the latter is important because it can account for many of the observed changes in the labor market without being accompanied by large changes either in trade and investment flows or in relative goods prices. As noted in chapter 1, the increased substitutability of low-skilled workers across borders affects three key ingredients of the employment relationship: the incidence of nonwage costs, volatility of earnings and hours worked, and bargaining in the workplace. I take up each in turn.

Incidence

Increased trade and investment opportunities make it more costly for workers to achieve a high level of labor standards and benefits. The costs of improved working conditions can no longer be shared with employers

---

4. See Leamer (1996) for a nice exposition.

5. This follows from the Le Chatelier-Samuelson principle. I thank Avinash Dixit for reminding me of the relevance of the principle in this context. Appendix A presents a simple model in which the elasticity of demand for domestic labor increases with the international mobility of physical capital.

Figure 2.1 Effect of openness on the distribution of the costs of labor standards between employers and workers

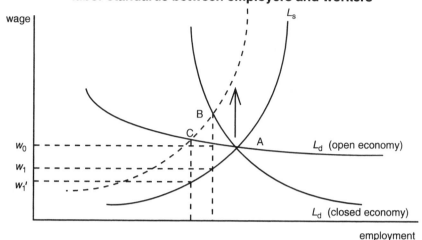

Imposition of a labor standard shifts the labor supply curve (L_s) up. In a closed economy, wages then fall from w_0 to w_1. In an open economy, wages fall from w_0 to w_1'.

with the same ease as before because employers are more sensitive to changes in such costs. The larger this elasticity of demand for labor, the higher the share of such costs that the workers themselves must bear.

The point can be seen using the supply-demand framework (figure 2.1). The initial labor-market equilibrium in the North is represented by point A, with wages at w_0. Now consider the consequences of raising labor standards—say, enhancing workplace safety. From the perspective of employers, labor standards can be viewed as a tax on employment. The result is a shift up in the effective labor supply curve (L_s) by an amount corresponding to the additional (per-worker) cost of introducing the standard. In the new equilibrium, as in the usual tax-incidence analysis, some of the additional cost will be borne by employers and the rest by workers. What determines how that cost is distributed between employers and workers is the elasticity of demand for labor. Two cases are shown in the figure—labor demand (L_d) in an open economy and in a closed one.

As figure 2.1 shows, the more elastic labor demand is (represented by the flatter open-economy demand curve), the greater the part of the cost increase workers must bear: wages fall from w_0 to w_1' rather than from w_0 to w_1. The reduction of employment in the affected industry is larger as well. Hence, in an integrated world economy, higher labor standards cost workers more in terms of both wages and jobs.

This relates to a common complaint that low labor standards in exporting countries pressure importing countries to adopt lower labor standards as well. This is the well-known race-to-the-bottom argument, according to which workers in the North will have to acquiesce in standards that are low enough to prevent footloose capital and employers from deserting them for the South.

The argument has surface appeal but is correct only in the limited sense that globalization alters the incidence of nonwage costs. The case against the race-to-the-bottom argument has been put well by Richard Freeman (1994a): Any country that wants higher labor standards can purchase them for itself, regardless of the level of standards in other countries, in one of the following three ways. First, a currency devaluation can be used to reduce domestic costs in foreign currency terms, thereby offsetting the loss in competitiveness. Second, there could be a downward adjustment in wages directly (which is the incidence point again). Third, the government can pay for the cost of higher labor standards, financed through an increase in taxes. Provided one or a combination of these approaches is followed, the presence of demanding labor standards does not put competitiveness and jobs at risk in rich countries. The race to the bottom need not take place.

Yet, as the incidence analysis shows, there is a sense in which globalization makes the race to the bottom a possibility. Freeman is correct, of course, that higher labor standards can be maintained if there is a willingness to pay for them. What increased openness to trade and foreign investment does, however, is render it more difficult for workers to make other groups in society, and employers in particular, share in the costs. Consider the three options mentioned earlier: devaluation, taxation, and wage cuts. As long as employers and capitalists have the option of moving (or importing from) abroad, they cannot be induced to take a hit in terms of real after-tax earnings.[6] Therefore, devaluation can work only insofar as it results in a disproportionate cut in take-home real wages. The same is true for taxation. One way or another, it is workers that must pay the lion's share of the cost.

Hence globalization makes it difficult to sustain the postwar bargain under which workers' pay and benefits steadily improved in return for labor peace and loyalty. It could be argued that this is appropriate insofar as it is *labor* standards, and hence an improvement in the working conditions for labor, that is at issue. Labor advocates, in turn, could point out that increased economic integration is undoing the implicit bargain with employers.

Volatility

The flattening of labor demand curves as a consequence of globalization results in greater instability in labor-market outcomes. Shocks to labor

---

6. To the extent that it remains costly to move abroad, employers will still share some part of the cost of worker benefits, but to a lesser degree than before.

Figure 2.2 Effect of openness on labor market's reaction to shocks

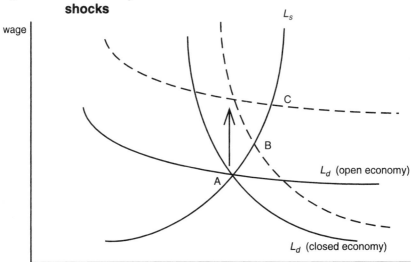

An increase in labor productivity shifts the labor demand curves (L_d) up in both closed and open economies, but the increase in wages and employment in the open economy, represented by the shift in equilibrium from A to C, is greater than in the closed economy.

demand—caused, for instance, by a sudden increase or decrease in labor productivity—now result in much greater volatility in both earnings and hours worked. This is important insofar as it can account directly for some of the widening wage inequality since the late 1970s, as well as for the increase in inequality *within* skill groups.

Let's consider the supply-demand framework again (figure 2.2). The initial labor-market equilibrium in an advanced industrial country is represented by point A. Two labor demand curves (L_d) are shown for this equilibrium: one for a closed economy and one for an open economy. The open-economy labor demand curve is the flatter, more elastic one. Consider the consequences of an exogenous shock to labor demand that a change in goods prices or labor productivity might produce, for example. As drawn, the shock is a positive one, so both labor demand curves shift up by an equal amount. For the closed economy, the new equilibrium is at point B, and for the open economy it is at point C. That is, there is a larger increase in wages and employment in the open economy than there is in the closed economy. Conversely, had the productivity shock been a negative one, wages and employment would have fallen by a greater amount in the open economy. In short, openness magnifies the effects of shocks on the labor market.

Table 2.1 Effect of increasing instability in earnings and employment, 1970-87

	Permanent variance				Transitory variance			
	1970-78	1979-87	Change	Percent change	1970-78	1979-87	Change	Percent change
Real annual earnings								
Whole sample	0.201	0.284	0.083	41	0.104	0.148	0.044	42
Workers with fewer than 12 years of education	0.175	0.272	0.097	55	0.106	0.208	0.102	96
Log weekly wage	0.171	0.230	0.059	35	0.075	0.101	0.026	35
Log of weeks worked	0.014	0.020	0.006	43	0.046	0.063	0.017	37

A significant increase in volatility in labor-market conditions has been well documented in the United States, a fact that apparently also accounts for an important part of the rise in wage inequality. Table 2.1 reports the findings of a study by Gottschalk and Moffitt (1994). It shows that between one-third and one-half of the widening wage distribution from the 1970s to the 1980s can be attributed to the increase in the short-term variance in earnings (i.e., the increase in the average worker's earnings variation from year to year). Between the two periods (1970-78 and 1979-87), the permanent variance of real annual earnings rose by 41 percent (from 0.20 to 0.28), reflecting the dispersion in permanent earnings. The transitory variance, which is roughly half as large as the permanent variance, rose by almost the same percentage amount (42 percent). This indicates that fully one-third of the widening of the measured earnings distribution has resulted from an increase in the instability of earnings. Moreover, the increase in short-term volatility nearly doubles for the least-skilled groups. (See the numbers for workers with less than 12 years of education, for whom demand has presumably become the most elastic.)

Recent evidence analyzed by Farber (1996) also suggests an increase in job insecurity in the 1990s compared with the 1980s. Farber found, for example, that the rate of job loss in 1991-93 (during a slack labor market but with a modest recovery in place) was even higher than that of the severe recession in the early 1980s.[7] The most dramatic increase in job loss rates appears for managers and workers in sales and administration,

---

7. The rate of job loss is defined, roughly, as the number of workers reporting to have lost at least one job during the period, divided by the number of workers in the relevant category.

although it is still craftspeople, operatives, and laborers who incur the highest rates overall. Hence there are indications that downsizing is having measurable consequences on the job security of middle managers.[8] Farber (1996, 33-34) summarizes his findings thus:

> The results are fairly clear cut. Rates of job loss are up relative to the standard of the last decade. And the increase has not been uniform. Older and more educated workers, while continuing to have lower rates of job loss than younger and less educated workers, have seen their rates of job loss increase more than those of other groups. . . . The costs of job loss are dramatic. Displaced workers have a substantial probability of not being employed at the survey date after displacement (about 36 percent on average).

Neither Farber nor Gottschalk and Moffitt analyze the causes of these changes, and they do not link them to globalization in particular. But the facts they document are consistent with a picture of labor markets in which greater openness to trade interacting with short-term fluctuations in labor demand (or labor productivity) has resulted in greater inequalities across and within skill groups and greater instability in wages and employment. Hence it is plausible that the deep sense of insecurity felt by participants in today's labor market is related to the fact that globalization has made their services much more easily substitutable than before.

A simple numerical exercise suggests that plausible increases in the elasticity of demand for labor can indeed account for the observed volatility in US labor markets. As figure 2.2 indicates, the extent to which wages and employment become more volatile in response to labor-productivity shocks depends on the elasticity of labor supply as well as the increase in the elasticity of labor demand. Assume that individual industries face a labor supply elasticity of 1 in the short to medium run. Assume further that globalization has resulted in an increase in the elasticity of demand for labor (again at the industry level) from -0.5 to -0.75—which is not a very large change and is in line with Slaughter's (1996) results. Then one can calculate that the standard deviation of wages and hours worked at the industry level would increase by 29 percent.[9] This number is commensurate with the figures in the last column of table 2.1 taken from Gottschalk and Moffitt 1994.

Bhagwati (1996, 14-16) has recently stressed another, related channel through which globalization may have aggravated job insecurity. He

---

8. A 1996 report by the Council of Economic Advisers (1996) reaches the same conclusions as Farber does.

9. To see this, let k stand for an index of labor productivity, w for wages, l for hours worked (all expressed as percentage changes) and ϵ and σ for the elasticities of labor demand and labor supply, respectively. Then w and l can be expressed as $w = [\epsilon/(\sigma + \epsilon)] k$ and $l = [\epsilon\sigma/(\sigma + \epsilon)] k$. Fixing σ at 1, the increase in the standard deviations of w and l, as ϵ goes from 0.5 to 0.75, can be calculated using these formulas.

points out that global economic integration has made competition in product markets itself more volatile:

> What we are facing now is a new and steadily encroaching reality where the nature of comparative advantage is becoming 'thin,' volatile, kaleidoscopic. . . . The margins of competitive advantage have . . . become thinner: a small shift in costs somewhere can now be deadly to your competitiveness.

This argument complements and augments the point that globalization makes the demand curve for labor more elastic (without any change in goods-market volatility). If, as Bhagwati argues, globalization also increases volatility in product markets, the effects are even larger.

Finally, increased churning in labor markets not only aggravates insecurity and inequality within skill categories, it can also exert downward pressure on the relative wages of less-educated workers as a whole and widen the skill premium. This is because less-educated workers fare considerably worse when they are displaced from a job than more educated workers. They experience both longer unemployment spells and larger wage cuts (relative to predisplacement earnings) upon reemployment. Farber (1996, 23) finds that "a [displaced] worker with a college education is about 18 percentage points more likely to be employed at the survey date than an otherwise-comparable worker with a high-school education." His results also suggest that a displaced high school dropout incurs a greater wage loss in his new job than a displaced college graduate (the differential is on the order of 7 percentage points—see Farber 1996, table 8). One reason for these disparities could be that job-specific skills constitute a larger component of earnings for less-educated workers than for college graduates (the latter having educational qualifications that are more transferable across firms or industries). Whatever the reason, the asymmetry in postdisplacement labor-market outcomes is an additional channel through which globalization, acting via increased labor-market turnover, can contribute to inequality.[10]

Bargaining

As mentioned previously, the greater substitutability of labor also alters the nature of bargaining between workers and employers and contributes to the weakening of unions. This part of the picture has received surprisingly little attention in the academic literature on trade and wages, primarily because the focus has typically been on perfectly competitive settings in which wages are determined in spot markets.[11] There is by now consid-

---

10. This point was first hypothesized by Bhagwati and Dehejia (1994, 56-57).

11. Borjas and Ramey (1994, 1995) are two significant exceptions. Richardson and Khripounova (1996) is a recent paper that has tackled this issue head on.

erable evidence, however, of the presence of labor rents in manufacturing industries (see in particular Katz and Summers 1989 and Blanchflower, Oswald, and Sanfey 1996). This evidence indicates that part of labor remuneration in these industries comes in the form of rent sharing with the employers.

To the extent that wages are determined in bargaining between workers and employers, an increase in the substitutability of workers results in a lower share of the enterprise surplus ending up with workers. A related consequence is that unions become weaker. The more substitutable workers in Akron are with those in Monterrey or Bombay, the less bargaining power they have and the lower the wage they will receive. In the words of Borjas and Ramey (1995, 1109), "[F]oreign competition in industries such as automobiles may have led to increased wage inequality not just by shifting workers from high wage sectors to low wage sectors, but also by changing the wage-setting behavior of the entire economy."

One can debate the quantitative significance of the decline in bargaining power engendered by the differential global mobility of employers versus employees. But there can be little doubt that this has changed the nature of employment contracts in many tradeable goods industries, and through example or spillover, in many nontradeable ones as well.

"At the end of the 1970s," according to Howell (1994), "firms began to fundamentally reassess their employment and wage-setting practices." Mitchell (1985) has documented a striking transformation in union contracts starting in the early 1980s, a transformation that is not well accounted for by either the disinflation of those years or the above-average unemployment rate. The transformation was reflected in wage freezes and cuts, which first showed up in a narrow range of industries in 1981 and then spread to others. Management appeared to be increasingly taking a harder stance. Mitchell calls this a "norm shift" in wage determination. While not all the sectors in which this happened were those that came under increased exposure to trade in the early 1980s (e.g., construction and retail food stores), many were (e.g., metal manufacturing, machinery, lumber and paper, aerospace).

The pattern set in the early 1980s survived even though the trade deficit was eventually reduced. In the words of Howell (1994):

> The undermining of traditional wage-setting institutions has lowered wages for those with the least bargaining power in the labor market, thus increasing inequality between skilled and unskilled workers. It may have also tended to increase wage inequality among workers in the same education, age, and gender group in the same industry. While the conventional view is that technological change has increased the demand for skill, leading to an increased premium for "unobserved skills" within these groups, it may be that the deinstitutionalization of the labor market has had a greater effect. Wage norms appear to have broken down within firms (as internal labor markets are opened up to external competition), within industries (as increasing competition causes differences among firms to become a more critical factor in wage outcomes), and among communities (as transporta-

tion and telecommunications facilitate the relocation of some, but not all, firms to lower wage areas).

Freeman (1996b) estimates that about one-fifth of the rise in US wage inequality is due to the decline in unionization. In Western Europe, where unions have remained stronger and the policy environment more supportive, the wages of the less skilled have not collapsed. But the price has been an increase in unemployment.

To many economists, the undermining of unions may not seem like such a bad thing, and this impression is plausibly strengthened by the European experience with unemployment. Indeed, from an efficiency standpoint, the weakening of unions, and of labor's bargaining abilities more generally, can have some benefits. But there is an often overlooked point here: these efficiency benefits are reaped only to the extent that employment *expands* in industries in which artificially high wages previously kept employment below efficient levels.[12] Has this actually happened? It is difficult to make a prima facie case that expanded trade has in fact led to more hiring in sectors such as steel and autos in the United States—sectors where monopsony wages were perhaps the most prevalent. And in the absence of such a case, the positive efficiency consequences of deunionization are in doubt. The first-order effect of trade appears to have been a redistribution of the enterprise surplus toward employers rather than the enlargement of that surplus.

In any case, bargaining is important not only in unionized industries. Even without unions and in the absence of other labor-market imperfections, the accumulation of job-specific skills creates a situation of bilateral monopoly between workers and employers *ex post*. In other words, job-specific skills are a form of rent, the distribution of which must be determined via bargaining within the enterprise. Anything that alters the relative bargaining power of the parties—such as globalization—can be expected to affect how the value of job-specific skills is distributed and how much accrues to the workers themselves. And to the extent that a larger share of low-skilled workers' remuneration derives from job-specific skills, as suggested previously, this will produce a differential effect that widens the wage gap between low-skilled and high-skilled workers.

Recapitulation

There is an important distinction between the two effects discussed in this chapter: the inward shift of the demand for low-skilled labor and the

---

12. This is because the efficiency costs of unions arise from there being too little employment in unionized industries, not from the high wages received by unionized workers per se—although of course the first is likely to be the consequence of the second. When unions are propped up by existing trade restrictions, this reduction in employment is actually not bad

increase in its elasticity. The first effect operates to any significant extent only when a country trades with another country that is considerably more abundant in low-skilled labor. That is why the empirical literature essentially focuses on trade with developing countries. The bulk of the advanced industrial countries' trade, which is with each other, has no bearing here because it takes place among countries with similar factor endowments and hence does not have any implications for relative demands for skilled and unskilled labor. Thus, this approach necessarily absolves the vast majority of trade from any responsibility for problems in the labor market.

But the focus on trade with (and immigration from) low-wage countries ignores the fact that less-skilled workers in Germany or France are also in competition with similar workers in the United Kingdom or the United States, markets with which the former countries are considerably more tightly integrated than they are with India or China. And while North-North trade may have little perceptible impact on the relative demand for unskilled labor, it certainly makes this demand more elastic in all countries involved. In other words, the increase in the elasticity of demand for labor is a much more general phenomenon. It is a direct consequence of international economic integration, regardless of economic structure and the identity of the trade partners.

Consider the following thought experiment. Suppose the rest of the world consisted of economies that are identical to the United States, both in terms of their relative factor endowments and levels of wealth. Since there would be no comparative advantage, economic integration would result in little trade (save, of course, for trade based on scale economies) and no change in relative prices. But the services of US workers would now become more easily substitutable with those of foreign workers, thanks to the possibilities of trade, migration, and capital outflows. Hence, while US labor would not face a reduction in demand (since the rest of the world is assumed to be no more labor-abundant than the United States), it would certainly be confronted with a demand that is more responsive to changes in its costs—that is, more elastic. This would affect workers' ability to bargain in the workplace, the incidence of nonwage costs workers must bear, and volatility of earnings and hours worked, as discussed above.

There are reasons, then, to think that the main impact of globalization on labor markets may well be the increase in the (actual or perceived) elasticity of demand for unskilled workers and not the reduction in this demand per se. That is, workers now find themselves in an environment in which they can be more easily "exchanged" for workers in other

---

from an efficiency standpoint because it counteracts the production-side distortion of the trade restriction, the latter being too high output (and employment) in the import-competing industry.

countries. For those who lack the skills to make themselves hard to replace, the result is greater insecurity and a more precarious existence.

While this argument is intuitive and consistent with the sentiments expressed by those on the front lines of labor markets, we need more systematic evidence to back it up. The only econometric studies of which I am aware are the preliminary studies by Slaughter (1996) and Richardson and Khripounova (1996), which suggest that the elasticity of demand for labor in the United States has increased since the 1960s. The other available evidence is largely impressionistic and anecdotal. Hence it is difficult to be more specific about the quantitative magnitudes involved. How much has international economic integration raised the elasticities of demand for low-skilled labor in the relevant markets? And how much of the increase in inequality, across and within groups, and in the short-term variance in earnings and employment can this factor account for? Since an elasticity concerns changes at the margin, these questions cannot be simply answered by looking at volumes of trade and immigration. Nor is there any reason to believe that an increase in the elasticity of demand for labor would be necessarily associated with changes in the relative price of labor-intensive goods.

The answer, therefore, is that we cannot be certain about the quantitative magnitudes. The basic research on these questions has yet to be undertaken. What we can say with some confidence is that a fuller accounting of the labor-market consequences of globalization is likely to yield a picture that gives globalization a much more significant billing than it habitually receives when the question is focused narrowly on the rise in the *average* skill premium and solely on perfectly competitive markets.

3

Tensions between Trade and Domestic Social Arrangements

International trade creates arbitrage in the markets for goods, services, labor, and capital. The tendency for prices to converge as a result is the source of the gains from trade. But trade often exerts pressure toward another kind of arbitrage as well: arbitrage in national norms and social institutions. This does not happen directly, through trade in these "norms" or "institutions," as with goods and services, but indirectly, by raising the social cost of maintaining divergent social arrangements. This is a key source of tension in globalization.

I begin with an extended example, that of child labor in international trade. I will use this example as a springboard for some generalizations about how trade connects—or disconnects, as the case may be—with domestic social norms and institutions. Child labor happens to be a convenient example for this purpose, but of course it is also an important case in its own right.

Laying Out the Issues: The Example of Child Labor

Consider the case of XYZ Corp., a hypothetical American mid-sized firm that manufactures shoes in Pleasantville, Ohio. Under increasing pressure from encroaching imports and with profit margins squeezed tight, the firm decides to lay off 300 of its workers in Pleasantville and to subcontract the more labor-intensive parts of its operation to a local firm in Honduras. Outsourcing reduces XYZ Corp.'s costs substantially, and profit margins recover. The laid-off workers in Pleasantville eventually find jobs elsewhere. But many have to move to other towns, and most have to take lower-paying jobs.

By the standards of international trade theory, this is a success story. International trade allows specialization according to comparative advantage, and the result is a larger economic pie for both the United States and Honduras. Trade economists would be quick to point out that the process is unlikely to occur without some distributional consequences, as in the above example. Indeed, in the standard models used by international economists, the distributional consequences of trade typically dwarf its net contribution to national income.[1] Compensation of the losers *could* take care of the problem, as the larger economic pie resulting from trade in principle allows the losers to be compensated in full while leaving the beneficiaries—who must share some of their gains—still better off. And this is indeed the first line of defense in the classroom and in most policy debates when the economist presents the case for gains from trade.

However, compensation rarely takes place in practice and never in full. There are good theoretical reasons, having to do with incomplete information, the impossibility of implementing lump-sum transfers, and the absence of a full set of tax/subsidy instruments, why this is so.[2]

But a much better defense of the distributional consequences of trade can be constituted along the following lines. Note first that preventing trade—that is, blocking XYZ Corp.'s outsourcing activities—also has a distributional effect: that of preventing XYZ's shareholders and remaining workers from raising their incomes. A number of considerations enter into how society evaluates these two distributional allocations—one with trade and one without—and therefore how it decides on whether trade is a good idea. One simple consideration is the relative size of the gains versus losses, as well as their incidence. We are much more likely to approve of a policy that creates large income benefits spread over a wide base than of a policy that creates a small net gain at the cost of a huge redistribution of income. Second, the identity of the gainers and losers matters as well. Rawlsian conceptions of justice, for example, imply that redistributions that enhance the well-being of the most disadvantaged groups should receive priority. Third, we could take a cue from the

---

1. Under typical parameters, lowering of a trade restriction will result in $5 or more of income being shuffled among different groups for every $1 of net gain. See Rodrik (1994) for further discussion. Many trade economists also believe in *dynamic* gains from trade—i.e., in higher growth rates resulting from more open trade policies. The theoretical presumptions on this, however, are not very strong, and one can easily come up with models to the contrary. Neither is the empirical evidence on the trade-growth linkage as strong as it is sometimes believed.

2. It is said that an economist is someone who sees something work in practice and wonders if it can also work in theory. This sentence is added for the benefit of the economist who fits the adage.

"prospect" theory in economics and weight losses more heavily than gains, which would result in a bias toward the status quo.

In market economies, perhaps the most significant test that is applied in determining whether distributional changes are socially acceptable is the following: is the change in question the consequence of individual actions that do not violate norms of fair play? In other words, is the distributional advantage obtained through *means* that society considers legitimate? If the answer is yes, we are likely to accept the consequences, even if some individuals or groups suffer as a result.[3] Take the case of technological innovation. An inventor who comes up with a new process or product through hard work and ingenuity is hailed as a hero, even if the invention displaces workers committed to the old technology. We would not dream of banning the light bulb to please candle makers!

Opening up to international trade is formally equivalent, in all economic respects, to technological progress. Both result in a larger economic pie at the possible cost of some redistribution of income.[4] If we presume that technological progress is good and ought to be encouraged rather than restricted, why not accept the same for liberalization of international trade as well? The analogy clarifies a central point: distributional implications alone, even if recognized to be adverse, do not provide a justification for imposing restrictions on foreign trade. This, I believe, is the central argument in favor of maintaining open borders to international commerce.

Note, however, that this defense of free trade is a contingent one. It requires, in particular, that the exchanges that create the gains from trade be consistent with the prevailing norms and rules of "fair play" at home. Returning to the analogy of technological progress, inventors who achieve their ends through lying, cheating, plagiarizing, or otherwise violating widely held domestic norms are reviled rather than celebrated.[5] Indeed, governments routinely interfere in R&D activities to ensure their consistency with social norms. Experimentation on human subjects and on animals is heavily regulated, for example. Ethical considerations impinge

---

3. In the concise wording of the philosopher Robert Nozick (1974, 151), "A distribution is just if it arises from another just distribution by legitimate means."

4. In the domestic context, we think of a "production function" as representing the technology through which intermediate inputs and primary factors are transformed into final goods. International trade is entirely analogous to such a production function: The goods that we sell abroad allow us to purchase imports in return, and hence our exports can be thought of as the inputs that get transformed into imports (the outputs). Prevailing international prices indicate the "input-output" coefficients used in this transformation. And, continuing the analogy, a terms-of-trade improvement (due, for example, to lower labor standards in a partner country) acts just like a technical advance in this technology by reducing the input-output coefficients.

5. In the economics field, another relevant example is the ban on insider trading. The ban is motivated less by efficiency considerations—which are difficult to construct and may even go in the opposite direction—than by considerations of fairness.

heavily on research in biotechnology. And over the last two centuries rich countries have developed labor legislation and standards that tightly circumscribe the nature of the production process. The bottom line is that once we are forced to provide a principled defense of free trade, there is no avoiding issues of fairness and legitimacy.

Perhaps ironically, libertarians, who are the staunchest defendants of free trade, would agree that the case for free trade is deep down a moral one. James Bovard of the Cato Institute, for example, makes this case strongly in arguing that government has no business restricting trade (1991): "Every trade restraint is a moral issue, forcibly sacrificing some Americans for the benefit of others." The unstated corollary is that removing a trade barrier reverses the sacrifices. Hence, strike out the term "forcibly," and I would agree with Bovard's statement. Where libertarians part company from most people, however, is in their belief that laissez-faire is the ultimate criterion for distributive justice—hence the use of the loaded term "forcibly" in the quote.

To draw the implications of the argument more concretely, let us return to the XYZ Corp. Suppose that some time after the firm has returned to profitability thanks to outsourcing, a journalist from Pleasantville visits the subcontracting plant in Honduras. He reports that the plant is a sweatshop, where 12-year-old children work under unsanitary and hazardous conditions. The news shocks the community. Picket lines are organized outside the headquarters of the firm, and after several days the president of the company announces that the subcontracting relationship with the Honduran firm has been terminated. He adds that XYZ will be hiring locally again.

What has just transpired is that vocal groups in Pleasantville have declared it unacceptable to displace adult American workers with 12-year-old children working under hazardous conditions. The message is: we do not accept this as a legitimate exchange and a fair way of imposing a burden on a segment of our society. Is this a good thing? And if yes, why not generalize the practice and pass legislation that bans all imports manufactured by child labor?[6] Doing so would be in conflict with the rules of the World Trade Organization, which has an exception on prison labor (Article XX[e]) but otherwise does not allow for discrimination among commodities or countries on the basis of differences in the mode of production.[7]

Most trade economists would also find it objectionable to impose trade restrictions on other countries because of differences in national practices

---

6. A bill proposed in the US Congress in 1995, the Child Labor Deterrence Act, aims to do precisely that.

7. For example, when the United States banned imports of Mexican tuna because Mexico had not taken steps to reduce the number of Eastern Pacific tropical dolphins killed due to tuna fishing, Mexico appealed to the General Agreement on Tariffs and Trade (GATT)

such as labor standards.[8] In one of the most thorough discussions of the issue, T. N. Srinivasan (1995) argues that introducing labor-standard concerns into the formulation of trade policy is a bad idea. Most of his objections have to do with the ineffectiveness of trade policy, or possibly its backfiring, where the well-being of workers in the exporting countries is concerned. For example, by denying the children working in the Honduran footwear industry access to the US market, XYZ could leave them in even more dire circumstances. Further, if individuals in the United States care about these children, they should make transfer payments to them rather than using such an indirect tool as trade policy. The conclusion of Srinivasan and many other economists is that demands for denying entry to exports made with child labor largely reflect US protectionist desires to keep competing imports out.

But while protectionist motives are apparent in many of the discussions on the "new" agenda for trade policy—over labor standards, environment, and competition policy—it would be a mistake not to recognize that they also reflect genuine discomfort in the importing countries with the moral or social implications of trade. I offer two bits of evidence. The first comes from a recent paper by Alan Krueger (1996). Krueger undertook an interesting test of the protectionism hypothesis by examining the sponsors of the Child Labor Deterrence Act. The proposed act would prohibit imports made by child labor. Such imports compete most directly with production in districts in which the labor force tends to be low-skilled. If the sponsors of the act were motivated chiefly by protectionist interests, one would expect them to be drawn disproportionately from such districts. In fact, Krueger found the opposite. The greater the proportion of high school dropouts in a district, the *lower* the likelihood that its representative would be a sponsor of the bill. Support for the act came instead from higher income districts and was apparently based on humanitarian rather than material concerns.[9]

The second bit of evidence can be derived from putting a twist on the XYZ story. Suppose that, instead of outsourcing, the company closes its

---

and won. Part of the rationale behind the GATT ruling was that the United States had applied a trade restriction on the basis of the process of production.

8. The original International Trade Organization charter was concerned with labor standards and trade. It had a whole article on fair labor standards (Article 7), which stated that "all countries have a common interest in the achievement and maintenance of fair labor standards related to productivity and thus in the improvement of wages and working conditions as productivity may permit." Further, "Unfair labor conditions, particularly in production for export, create difficulties in international trade, and, accordingly, each member shall take whatever action may be appropriate and feasible to eliminate such conditions within its territory." So these issues were very much on the minds of the architects of the postwar international economic system.

9. Krueger also applied his framework to the congressional votes over the North American Free Trade Agreement (NAFTA) and the World Trade Organization (WTO). His findings

main plant in Pleasantville, opens up a domestic sweatshop near the Mexican border, and brings in 12-year-old children from Honduras as temporary migrants. From the standpoint of economic outcomes, this solution to the firm's competitive problem is indistinguishable from the previous one of outsourcing through trade. The well-being of all the parties—the laid-off workers, the firm's shareholders, and the Honduran children—are affected in exactly the same way.

The difference in practice is that taking this option would break the law. Labor laws in the advanced industrial countries make only a limited number of exceptions to the rule that migrant workers—temporary or otherwise—have to work under the same rules as those that apply to domestic workers. To be sure, the rules are frequently flouted. But when they are and the infractions are discovered, the public outcry is loud and the transgressors are punished. This demonstrates, in my view, the prevailing norm that it is not acceptable to reduce the living standards of American workers by taking advantage of labor practices that are vastly below those enshrined in US standards.

Interestingly, the vast majority of the economists who have no difficulty with the outsourcing example would also accept that it is not good public policy to relax labor standards for migrant workers to the point of allowing sweatshop conditions. Clearly, there is an inconsistency between these two positions. There seems to be greater coherence in the behavior of the lay public, which reacts with equal outrage to the two versions of the parable—outsourcing versus migration—than in the precepts of the economists.

Let me emphasize two key features of my argument. First, there is no conflict with comparative advantage per se, as long as it is founded on processes that are perceived as legitimate at home. That is why, contrary to economists' thinking, there is a difference between comparative advantage created by differences in relative factor endowments or preferences and that created by institutional choices that conflict with norms in the importing country. Second, the argument does not rely on Americans caring greatly about the well-being of the Honduran children; it only presumes that Americans care for other Americans and that there are social norms regarding what is an acceptable manner of imposing a burden on others.

But what about imports that do not compete directly with domestic production and therefore do not displace American workers? Does this mean that the manner in which these imports are manufactured—whether they use child labor or defile the environment—is of no consequence for trade policy in the importing countries? Of course, some if not most Americans also care about the plight of underage workers or about environmental conditions in the rest of the world. But when such global

---

there are consistent with the self-interest motive. Representatives from low-skill districts were less likely to vote in favor of NAFTA or the WTO.

humanitarian motives—as opposed to domestic distributional concerns—are the driving force, there is a good case to be made that they carry very little implication for trade policy.

The reason is simple: it is quite unclear whether trade policies, and import restrictions in particular, are a good instrument to advance the cause of labor or the environment among one's trading partners. The arguments, such as T. N. Srinivasan's above, that there are often far better instruments to achieve these global-humanitarian goals—ranging from allowing migration to providing foreign technical and financial assistance—have to be answered before a good case can be mounted for interfering with trade. Furthermore, as mentioned earlier, restrictive trade policies in the advanced countries often worsen the situation of those in the exporting countries they were designed to help. The alternative for child workers in export industries, for example, may often be worse (e.g., prostitution).

In the case of *noncompeting* imports, then, the standard economics argument on behalf of free trade is on much more solid ground. However, even in this case, there may be other influences on domestic social arrangements, to be discussed shortly, that need to be considered.

Trade and "Blocked Exchanges"

Every society has restrictions, moral or legal, on what kinds of markets are allowed. Individuals are never completely free to sign certain kinds of contracts. The political philosopher Michael Walzer has called these "blocked exchanges." In the United States, such blocked exchanges cover a number of areas, including the sale of human beings and of political office. They also cover "trades of last resort" or "desperate" exchanges, as illustrated by laws on the eight-hour day, minimum wages, and health and safety regulations (see Walzer 1983, 100-03, for an exhaustive listing). Some of these restrictions, such as the prevention of enslavement, are hardly controversial. Others, such as minimum wage laws, are more so. Moreover, norms for what should be restricted vary across countries and also change over time. The point is simply that blocked exchanges are part of the social arrangements of every society.

The history of US labor law nicely illustrates how blocked exchanges come into being and evolve. During the early part of the 20th century, there was much resistance to legislation that would reduce hours and improve working conditions. In 1905, the Supreme Court struck down a New York statute prohibiting the employment of bakery employees for more than 60 hours per week (*Lochner v. New York*). The Court's opinion was based on the idea that voluntary exchanges ought not be restricted. In the Court's words, the New York statute was "an illegal interference with the rights of individuals, both employers and employees, to make contracts regarding labor upon such terms as they may think best" (cited in Sandel 1996, 41). On similar reasoning, the Court also struck down a law that set minimum wages for women and one that prohibited contracts allowing workers to be fired for joining a union.

Facing a threat by President Franklin D. Roosevelt to pack the Court, the Supreme Court reversed course in 1937. In a decision that year (*West Coast Hotel Co. v. Parrish*), it upheld a minimum wage law for women. Its justification this time was that it is proper for legislatures to address sweatshop conditions, and in particular to consider unequal bargaining powers between employer and employee. As the Court put it, women's "bargaining power is relatively weak, and . . . they are the ready victims of those who would take advantage of their necessitous circumstances." Consequently, it was proper to redress this inequality through legislation and restrictions on the individual's right of contract. This watershed case opened the door for subsequent labor legislation that greatly expanded the scope of regulation in the workplace.

Hence US laws since the 1930s have recognized that restrictions on "free contract" are legitimate in the case of unequal bargaining power. But consider now a different source of asymmetric bargaining power, one created by trade and capital mobility and discussed in the previous chapter: employers can move abroad but employees cannot. One could argue that by generating an inequality in bargaining power globalization helps undermine 60 years of labor legislation and thus the social understanding those laws represent. After all, there is little substantive difference between domestic workers being able to compete against their fellow workers by agreeing to work 12-hour days, earn below-minimum wages, and agree to be fired if they join a union—all of which would be illegal under US law—and foreign workers doing the same. If society is unwilling to accept the former, why should it countenance the latter?[10]

There is no clear-cut or categorical answer to this question. There are different values and interests to trade off, including the gains and losses at stake and contending conceptions of "fair" competition. My point is simply that trade impinges on domestic society in ways that can conflict with long-standing social contracts to protect citizens from the relentlessness of the free market.

The New Trade Issues and Demands for "Fair Trade"

"Restructuring nations—at least, certain aspects of nations," writes Ruggie (1995, 510) "is what trade disputes increasingly have come to be

---

10. Note that appealing to national sovereignty and the general unacceptability under international law of attempts to impose domestic legislation on other countries does not get us out of this conundrum. In fact, it cuts the other way. National sovereignty implies

about." That is indeed the common theme that runs through the gamut of the so-called new issues on the WTO's agenda. Whether it is labor standards, environmental policy, competition policy, or corruption, differences in domestic practices have become matters of international controversy. Conflicts arise both when these differences create trade—as in the cases of child labor or lax environmental policies—and when they allegedly reduce it—as with *keiretsu* practices in Japan. Gone are the days when trade policy negotiations were chiefly about interference with trade at the border—tariffs and nontariff barriers. The central trade issues of the future are "deep integration," involving policies inside the borders, and how to manage it. As a *New York Times* editorial (approvingly) put it in connection with the Kodak-Fuji dispute on access to the photographic film market in Japan, "The Kodak case asks the WTO, in effect, to pass judgment on the way Japan does business" (11 July 1996, A22).

Economists have ridiculed the notions of "fair trade" and of "leveling the playing field" that lie behind many of these initiatives. But once it is recognized that trade has implications for domestic norms and social arrangements and that its legitimacy rests in part on its compatibility with these, such notions are not so outlandish; they address the concerns to which trade gives rise. Free trade among countries with very different domestic practices requires either a willingness to countenance the erosion of domestic structures or the acceptance of a certain degree of harmonization (convergence). In other words, some degree of international harmonization (convergence) may be necessary for the gains from trade to be reaped.

If this is the appropriate context in which demands for "fair trade" or "leveling the playing" field have to be understood, it should also be clear that policymakers often take too many liberties in justifying their actions along such lines. Most of what passes as "unfair trade" in US antidumping proceedings, for example, is no more than standard business practice (such as pricing over the product cycle or pricing down to average variable cost during market downturns), and no less in the United States than in other countries. Too often, the US government itself engages in the policies that it labels unfair when undertaken by others. The US government was outraged when the European Community banned the import of American beef produced with growth hormones in December 1988, apparently without scientific evidence that the beef hormones had adverse effects on humans. At the time it maintained a ban on imports of German ham on the grounds that it was unsafe for Americans (for this and similar examples, see Bovard 1991).

Hence, while there may not be a very sharp dividing line between what is fair and what is not in international trade, one clear sign that

the ability of each country to sever its trade links with others if trade undermines its sovereign choices at home.

unprincipled protectionism lies at the root of a trade complaint made on fairness grounds is the prevalence of identical or similar practices within the domestic economy of the plaintiff. Fairness cannot be kept out of the thinking on trade policy, but neither can it be used as an excuse for trade restrictions when the practice in question does not conflict with domestic norms *as revealed by actual practice.*

In addition, even when such conflicts are created, fairness considerations can at best justify only the use of trade restrictions at home (to "protect" our own values and institutions); they do *not* warrant any attempt to impose our norms or institutions on others. For instance, we might perhaps be justified in keeping Fuji out of the US market if Fuji's behavior grossly violates US norms and business ethics. However, we would not be justified in insisting that Japan change its practices so that Kodak can compete in Japan with Fuji on a level playing field.

Integration and Social Policy in Europe

Among advanced industrial countries, the integration of markets for goods and services is furthest along in Europe. The process of integration within the European Union provides an interesting case study of the tensions between trade and domestic social arrangements.

Discussions of harmonization have a long history in Europe, going back to the days before the creation of the European Economic Community (EEC).[11] The Treaty of Rome (1958) establishing the EEC has numerous clauses related to the harmonization of social policies in the name of assuring fair play and equalizing conditions of competition. Harmonization was called for in two specific areas: equal pay for men and women (Article 119) and paid holiday schemes (Article 120). France demanded the equal pay clause, as it already had legislation requiring equality of pay (while other countries did not). According to Sapir (1996), the French government feared that its textile industry (where a disproportionate number of workers are women) would be jeopardized in the absence of harmonization. In addition, a separate protocol stated that working hours and overtime rates were to converge with the levels prevailing in France in 1956 by the end of the first stage of the common market (31 December 1961). If the convergence were to fail to take place, France would be allowed to undertake protective measures.

In any event, these clauses appear to have had little practical effect. For example, the application of Article 119 on equal pay was repeatedly postponed, and it was not until 1975 that a directive in this area was adopted. As Sapir (1996) notes, the period 1958-73 has been called one of benign neglect as far as social policy is concerned. He ascribes this to the

---

11. This account of the history of EU harmonization is based on Sapir (1996).

high degree of social and economic homogeneity among the six original members of the EEC and to the rapid amelioration of living standards during these years. These factors, he argues, were crucial in "warding off pressures ... in favor of harmonization" in the early years (Sapir 1996, 544).

Since the mid-1970s, however, greater heterogeneity and slower growth have increased pressure for harmonization. After 1975 a flurry of directives were adopted on equal pay, labor law, and working conditions, but Sapir (1996) concludes that their scope remained limited. The movement gained force with the agreement on the Single European Act in December 1985 and especially with the adoption of the Social Charter by all member states except the United Kingdom in December 1989. As part of the Single European Act, two new articles on social policy were added to the Treaty of Rome, one on occupational health and safety standards and another on collective bargaining. And as a result of the Social Charter, the EC Commission developed a detailed action program containing close to 50 initiatives, many of which have been adopted. In the words of the Commission, the action program aims inter alia at "reducing disparities between Member States without interfering in the comparative advantage of the less-developed regions" (Commission of the European Communities 1993, 10). The fear of "social dumping" from new members, particularly Portugal and Spain, appears to have played a crucial role in these developments.[12] In 1993, the European Commission took the view that "competition within the Community on the basis of unacceptably low social standards, rather than the productivity of enterprises, will undermine the economic objectives of the Union" (Commission of the European Communities 1993, 59-60).

The United Kingdom, under Conservative governments, has been the main opponent of these moves toward social harmonization. Prime Minister John Major expressed the difference in values that the British government brought to the Community:

> Europe can have the social charter. We shall have employment.... Let Jacques Delors accuse us of creating a paradise for foreign investors; I am happy to plead guilty (cited in Leibfried and Pierson 1995, 49).

The United Kingdom argued instead for a decentralized system of rule making and "competition among rules" to allow for the emergence of national standards more conducive to superior economic and social out-

---

12. An Interdepartmental Working Party appointed by the European Commission defined social dumping in 1988 as "the fear that national social progress will be blocked or, worse, that there will be downward pressure on social conditions (wages, level of social protection, fringe benefits, etc.) in the most advanced countries, simply because of th[e] competition ... [from] certain [EEC] countries, where average labour costs are significantly lower" (cited in Sapir 1996, 559).

comes. Even though these two conceptions of social policy for an integrated Europe obviously differ a great deal, they share a common feature that is particularly relevant here. The system of "competition among rules," just like harmonization, implies eventual convergence—in this case through the competitive process of "good" rules driving out the "bad."

Sapir concludes that "the Social Charter and the implementing action programme do not appear to have added much in the way of 'social harmonization'—except in the area of occupational health and safety" (1996, 561). That the social dimension of European integration has led to only modest results to date is a widely shared conclusion. But as emphasized by Leibfried and Pierson (1995), that is not to say that integration has not had a significant impact on social policies in member states. While agreements among member states or actions by the Commission may have played a limited role, the interpretation of market compatibility requirements by the European Court of Justice (ECJ) has led to an unmistakable erosion of national sovereignty in the social field. The ECJ has delivered decisions on more than 300 cases on social policy coordination, and such cases account for a growing proportion of a caseload that has increased from 34 in 1968 to 553 in 1992 (Leibfried and Pierson 1995, 51). The thrust of these decisions has been to require that national social policies not restrict the free movement of goods, services, and individuals. In the words of Leibfried and Pierson (1995, 51): "The EU's social dimension is usually discussed as a corrective to market building, but it has proceeded instead as part of the market-building process."

For example, the ECJ has ruled that labor mobility requires identical social welfare benefits to be made available to all EU nationals employed in a member country; member states can no longer target welfare benefits at their citizens only. Similarly, a national government is no longer the sole authority on whether claims for benefits are to be accepted or not; decisions on eligibility made by administrative bodies in other member states may have to be complied with. The use of tax policy to revive economic activity in depressed regions, such as the Italian government's efforts to attract investment to the Mezzogiorno, has also become circumscribed on the grounds that this constitutes "unfair competition."[13] Harmonization may be too ambitious a term to describe this largely Court-based activity. Liebfried and Pierson (1995, 65) prefer to call it "an incremental, rights-based homogenization of social policy."

This brief account of the European Union points to a number of conclusions. First, it is considerably easier to integrate economically when there are shared norms among countries regarding domestic institutions such as labor relations or social welfare systems. Second, as integration deepens,

---

13. For these and other examples, with extensive discussion, see Leibfried and Pierson (1995, 50-65).

it becomes more difficult for countries to adopt or maintain social recipes that differ from those of their trade partners. Third, even within Europe, where there is substantial convergence in income levels and social practices—at least compared with the rest of the world—it has proved difficult to strike the right balance between expanding economic integration and providing governments with room for maneuver on the social front.

Maastricht, the French Strikes, and the Social Dimension

The widespread fear in Europe that economic integration will undermine prevailing social protection schemes is exemplified by the debates surrounding the Maastricht criteria and their implementation. Characteristically, the European governments (with the exception again of the United Kingdom) annexed a Protocol on Social Policy to the main text of the Maastricht treaty to underscore their intention to proceed on a social as well as economic path. The main contribution of the protocol is that it now allows the European Union to adopt initiatives in the social field by qualified majority voting instead of unanimity as before. Nonetheless, the Maastricht requirements on fiscal policy have called into question long-standing social policies in the member states. Consequently, Maastricht has had rough sailing, particularly in those countries in which it was subjected to a referendum. In June 1992 the Danes voted to reject the treaty, and in September of the same year the French came very close to doing so.[14] In Denmark, "[a]ccording to exit polls, the single most important reason for the negative vote . . . was the fear that the Danish social security system would be negatively affected by its integration with the other social security systems. . ." (Perotti 1996, 1).[15]

Opposition to Maastricht reached its highest point in the French strikes during the fall and winter of 1995. An account of these strikes makes a good cautionary tale about the social instability and disruption that is perhaps in store for other countries if the issues raised here are not addressed. The widespread popular support of these strikes in France, going beyond those whose interests were immediately at stake, is indicative of the deep nerve that the conflict between international integration and domestic institutions has struck.

The task of fulfilling the Maastricht treaty's fiscal criterion had fallen to President Jacques Chirac, inaugurated in May 1995, and his prime

---

14. In Ireland, the treaty was approved by a comfortable majority. A second referendum was held in Denmark in May 1993 after the Danish government obtained several concessions in the application of the treaty to Denmark, and the second vote resulted in ratification.

15. A similar concern was voiced by many Canadians in relation to the free trade agreement with the United States.

minister, Alain Juppé.[16] In 1995, France's public-sector deficit stood at nearly 5 percent of GDP, substantially larger than the 3 percent mark set by the treaty. Because countries were to qualify in 1998 based on 1997 figures, a reduction of the deficit by over one-third in only two years was required.

A serious attack on the deficit meant cuts in the country's social security system, which marked its 50th anniversary in October 1995 and represents half of all public-sector spending. Over the last 50 years, France has created an elaborate system of social protections, which have taken on the status of *acquis sociaux*, or acquired social rights. The unions and the French people generally have aggressively defended this system over the years, and it is not difficult to understand why. France's public health service, one of the most costly in the world, combines free care with freedom of choice: patients can visit virtually any doctor or specialist as often as they like and be reimbursed by the public health fund. All citizens are guaranteed free education through university. Employers are required to provide five weeks of vacation, and workers in high-stress jobs, such as medicine, receive nine weeks. All mothers, regardless of income or marital status, receive subsidies for each child. Larger, poorer families can receive paid holidays, including transportation to a resort, subsidized apartments, and dishwashers and washing machines (*New York Times*, 20 December 1995, A14). In addition, a major source of the social security deficit is the generous pension provisions granted government employees. Unlike private-sector workers, who must work 40 years to be eligible for a pension, civil servants can retire with a pension after 37½ years, and railroad workers can retire with a pension at age 50. Furthermore, pensions are calculated based on employees' earnings in their final six months, allowing many workers to artificially inflate their pensions by working overtime during that period.

Prime Minister Juppé first outlined the government's proposed measures to confront the deficit in a series of meetings with labor leaders in late August and early September 1995. The proposed budget was to impose a new 0.5 percent income tax to pay for the accumulated health and pension deficits, increase health care contributions for the retired and unemployed, shift control of the health care system from the unions to the Parliament, and require public employees to work for 40 years to be eligible for a pension.

The first sign of broad-based unrest was a one-day protest strike on 10 October in opposition to government plans to freeze civil service salaries in 1996. Fifty-seven percent of civil servants stayed away from work in a strike that involved 5 million workers and spread to state-sector industries including transportation, electricity, the postal service, and telecommuni-

---

16. The rest of this section relies heavily on an account prepared by Matthew Maguire.

cations. The strike, which effectively shut down the country for 24 hours, was the largest since 1981.

Despite the opposition, Juppé announced his package of spending cuts and tax increases to a session of the National Assembly, France's lower house, on 14 November. The vote, which he called one of confidence in his government, was 463 to 87 in favor of the program. The unions moved quickly to organize large-scale opposition, and on 24 November, the railway workers' unions launched a nationwide strike. On 29 November, they were joined by utility workers, who feared the breakup of the state electric power monopoly (*New York Times*, 30 November 1994, A15).

Support for the protesters among the general public was significant, even though less than 10 percent of French private-sector employees are unionized. A poll published in *Le Parisien* on 2 December showed 62 percent of respondents backing the strikers (*New York Times*, 3 December 1995, 20)—this despite the fact that the strike was essentially shutting down whole sectors of the economy. Parisian workers found their commutes taking up to four hours each way as traffic slowed to a standstill, and bicycles became the new status symbol.

The government initially stood firm. But the strike, initially to have been a short-term measure, continued and broadened. On 2 December, French union leaders called for a strike of all salaried workers, and air transport workers, telephone company employees, and truck drivers joined the walkout. As the strike entered its second week, the franc weakened due to investor fears of a government cave-in. The government declared its willingness to enter discussions with the unions but vowed to press forward with its welfare reform plans. By 7 December, over a third of all public employees were on strike, Juppé was burned in effigy in Bordeaux, where he is mayor, and a poll showed that 53 percent of respondents believed Juppé was wrong not to withdraw the austerity program (*New York Times*, 8 December 1995, A14).

The government, showing a new flexibility, named a mediator and offered discussions with the public employee unions. On 11 December, the government was forced to concede to the railway union on the pension issue, a concession that was extended to all public employees on 12 December. By 15 December, most of the unions had voted to return to work. However, the unions continued to insist on retraction of the new tax and health care cost-control proposals and planned continued demonstrations. On 21 December, Juppé promised "dialogue, consultation, and negotiation" at a "social summit" with labor and business leaders. He agreed to cut payroll taxes as a job creation measure and to impose a moratorium on tax increases, but only after a new system of paying for the health insurance and pension systems was agreed to in 1996. He refused to put off an increase set for 1 January (*New York Times*, 22 December 1995, A7). In January, Juppé secured validation from the Constitutional Council of a law allowing him to enact his social security reforms by decree.

The cost of the strikes to the French economy was tremendous. On 19 December the government estimated it at between 0.4 and 0.5 percent of quarterly GDP. But the strikes expressed a clear desire on the part of a sizable portion of the country not to sacrifice social protections to trade. "The French do not want to live like Anglo-Saxons," according to Marc Blondel, head of the Workers Force union, which was a primary mover behind the strikes (*San Francisco Chronicle*, 21 December 1995, B2). Or as one citizen stated, "I think most French people want France's values to be decided by this spirit, not by cold, remote, economic summits that speak of deficits and competition. That was the message of the strikes" (*New York Times*, 20 December 1995, A14).

Do Differences in National Institutions Have Effects on Trade?

Before the ink was dry on the Maastricht treaty, an event occurred that seemed to verify fears that economic integration would come at the cost of social regress. Hoover Europe, the subsidiary of the American company, announced in January 1993 that it was closing its plant in Burgundy, France, and relocating to Scotland. The company's decision was apparently motivated by the fact that unions in Scotland were ready to accept terms that were decidedly more flexible than those in France. As Sapir (1996, 563) puts it,

> The Hoover affair rapidly became the symbol of the debate on the danger of "social dumping" inside the integrated European market. It was probably the first instance of enterprise relocation inside the Community that attracted massive media and political attention. It was the perfect case, pitting France, the champion of "social harmonization" and the Social Charter, against the United Kingdom, the champion of "competition among rules" and opponent of the Social Charter.

Decisions of this type—where to produce, who to buy from—are made daily by managers of global corporations. Any labor advocate in the United States can provide a long list of cases in which firms previously based in the United States have moved south of the border, allegedly to take advantage of a less costly labor force of near-equal productivity. In comparison with most of Western Europe, of course, the United States is hardly a workers' haven, which sometimes makes for a reverse flow. BMW's decision to produce in South Carolina, for example, was motivated in part by the significant savings in labor costs.

Anecdotes of this kind are plentiful, but systematic evidence is harder to get. The difficulty with the anecdotes is that they don't tell us whether the chief responsibility for trade and investment flows lies with their underlying economic and structural determinants—relative factor endowments, productivities, consumer preferences, market size—or with differences in social arrangements, which can sometimes be controversial and construed as unfair. There is a difference between a US firm paying 50 cents an hour for a worker abroad who is one-tenth as productive as a US worker and paying the same for a worker who is equally productive.

So do differences in social institutions really make much difference in practice for trade? The theoretical case that they should is impeccable. After all, if cross-country differences in, for example, labor standards or environmental regulations can be treated "just like" any other determinant of comparative advantage—and this is the conventional economic approach to these matters—these differences must have implications for trade flows. The real question therefore is not "do they?" but "how much?" and "for what sorts of products and services?"

While social policies generate much heat, there is remarkably little quantitative evidence on their trade implications. In a recent paper, Alesina and Perotti (1995) undertook one of the few rigorous analyses in the context of the countries of the Organization for Economic Cooperation and Development (OECD). They hypothesize that more generous social welfare systems will be associated with lower competitiveness, defined as the inverse of unit labor costs relative to other countries. This is because pension or unemployment benefits have to be financed, in part, by payroll taxes. Workers can pass on some of the costs to employers (more when unionized), which in turn results in a loss in "competitiveness," reduction in exports, and an increase in unemployment. Alesina and Perotti's empirical results confirm the story. They find that "when taxes on labor increase by 1% of GDP from their sample average of about 24%, unit labor costs in countries with an intermediate degree of centralization [in labor-market institutions] increase by up to 2.5% relative to competitors" (Alesina and Perotti 1995, 4-5).

In the area of labor standards, the relationship between standards and trade has been examined in Rodrik (forthcoming). Using a wide range of labor-standard indicators, such as ratification of ILO Conventions and US Department of Labor reports on child labor problems, I focused the empirical analysis on three questions: Do labor standards affect labor costs? Do labor standards affect comparative advantage, and thereby trade flows? Do labor standards affect foreign direct investment? There was evidence in the affirmative on all three counts, although not always in the direction expected.

With regard to labor costs, in a cross-section of countries lax labor standards were associated with lower costs (expressed in dollar terms), after controlling for productivity. Moreover, the estimated effects were large, implying that the economic magnitude of the effects is significant as well. For example, an increase of one step in my measure of child labor (for example, moving from no child labor legislation to having such legislation) is associated with an increase in annual labor costs of $4,849 to $8,710. This is very large, perhaps implausibly so. However, child labor practices are likely to be indicative of a much wider range of shortcomings in labor standards. Consequently, the parameter estimates are probably an indication of the aggregate effect of all of these.

Turning next to trade flows, I found in a sample of developing countries that a measure of comparative advantage in labor-intensive goods—the ratio of textile and clothing exports to other exports, excluding fuels— was associated with indicators of labor standards in the expected manner: the more relaxed the standard, the larger the revealed comparative advantage in labor-intensive goods. Finally, investment by majority-owned US affiliates in manufacturing was also associated with indicators of labor standards, but not in the direction that is commonly claimed: countries with poor labor standards received less foreign investment than would have been predicted on the basis of their other characteristics. Taking these two results together leads to the hypothesis that poor labor standards result in outsourcing and subcontracting, but not majority-owned foreign investments.

Environmental policy is one area in which there has been substantial empirical research focused on the consequences of regulations on manufacturing "competitiveness" and trade. Pollution abatement costs in the advanced industrial countries are currently nonnegligible, and in the range of 1 to 2 percent of GDP for countries such as the United States, Germany, France, and the United Kingdom. Moreover, these costs vary greatly across manufacturing industries, from 25 percent of total capital expenditures in petroleum and coal products in the United States to less than 1 percent in printing and publishing (Jaffee et al. 1995, table 6). Jaffee et al. also survey the empirical evidence and report some evidence that pollution-intensive production has migrated to developing countries, but they find few studies that have concluded environmental regulations to be a significant determinant of competitiveness or comparative advantage. The evidence on plant location within the United States suggests that even relatively large differences in regulations have mild effects on siting. Hence, they conclude that "there is relatively little evidence to support the hypothesis that environmental regulations have had a large adverse effect on competitiveness, however that elusive term is defined" (Jaffee et al. 1995, 157). They attribute this finding to difficulties in measuring the impact of environmental regulations, to the fact that, in all but a few industries, complying with such regulations still constitutes a small share of total costs, and to similarities in practices among industrial countries.

In the area of industrial policies, Japan has received the most scrutiny. It is distinctive among the advanced countries in that it engages in low amounts of intra-industry trade and its imports of manufactured goods are a relatively small fraction of GDP (Bergsten and Noland 1993). There has been much controversy over whether differences in Japan's industrial structures and industrial-policy traditions have been responsible for these distinctive traits of Japanese trade—see, for example, the exchange between Lawrence (1993) and Saxonhouse (1993). Econometric studies on the relationship between trade flows and factor endowments have yielded ambiguous results and in any case do not speak to the question of why, if at all, Japan is different.

Lawrence's (1991) study on the *keiretsu* is one of the rare econometric studies analyzing the consequences of Japanese industrial structures. The term *keiretsu* refers to a network of affiliated firms, either within a single industry or across a range of industries. Outsiders often see these networks as a deterrent to imports and as an unfair trade practice. Lawrence attempts to distinguish empirically between two contending views of *keiretsu*. One view is that they are simply an efficiency-enhancing arrangement, with no discriminatory effect on imports. He reasons that, under this hypothesis, *keiretsu*-dominated sectors should have both lower imports and higher exports. The second view is that *keiretsu* do act as import barriers, in which case their presence should be associated with reduced imports but not necessarily higher exports. His findings suggest that the *keiretsu* indeed reduce imports, and that higher exports are (weakly) associated only with "vertical" *keiretsu*. Moreover, the estimated effects are large. High shares of *keiretsu* sales in an industry are associated with reductions in the import share of consumption by half. A more recent study by Noland (forthcoming) reports broadly similar findings.

Finally, a recent paper by Hines (1995) is noteworthy in that it has documented how national differences in tolerance toward corrupt trade practices can have implications for investment flows. In the wake of the Watergate scandal, the United States passed the Foreign Corrupt Practices Act (FCPA) of 1977, which makes it illegal for US businesses to pay bribes to foreign government officials. Until recently, other developed countries did not have similar legislation, even allowing in some cases tax deductibility of illicit payments.[17] The question Hines posed was whether this difference handicapped American businesses in countries where corruption is rampant. The answer he reached was a definite yes. Hines found that US investment activity in countries in which government officials routinely accept bribes showed "unusual" declines after 1977. The same was true for US aircraft exports and joint-venture activities as well. Hence US businesses lost ground in the more corrupt countries to firms from other developed countries not handicapped by similar domestic legislation.

---

17. In 1996, an OECD agreement recommended putting an end to this discrepancy.

Recapitulation

Differences in national choices of social arrangements have implications for trade and investment flows. These flows in turn impinge on domestic social arrangements elsewhere. I have argued here that trade is controversial on both accounts.

The most favorable argument on behalf of free trade is that it acts just like technological progress, expanding the economic pie, albeit at some distributional cost occasionally. Since governments routinely interfere in deciding what kind of technologies are permissible domestically, so as to take into account social costs or national norms, it is difficult to make a hard-line case as to why international trade should be categorically exempt from this same kind of approach. Trade restrictions will not generally be the most appropriate or efficient way to deal with the consequences of eroding domestic norms and institutions. But neither should we treat trade liberalization as an end in itself, without regard to how it affects broadly shared values at home.

Indeed, there are areas such as slave labor and prison labor where a certain degree of international convergence in norms has resulted in multilateral trade rules being written to reflect them. The much tougher cases are those in which no such convergence has taken place. The challenge for the international trading system will be to accommodate national preferences in this area without a free-for-all that could degenerate into blanket protectionism. A starting point is to recognize that nations do have legitimate reasons for worrying about what globalization does to their norms and social arrangements.[18] The final chapter will discuss some guiding principles on how to proceed from there.

---

18. Interestingly, this point is related to one of the arguments Keynes made in his advocacy of self-sufficiency in trade in a famous article in 1933. After discussing how different countries were each striving for what he called "new modes of political economy," he wrote: "We do not wish . . . to be at the mercy of world forces working out, or trying to work out, some uniform equilibrium according to the ideal principles . . . of *laissez-faire* capitalism. . . . [T]he policy of an increased national self-sufficiency is to be considered not as an ideal in itself but as directed to the creation of an environment in which other ideals can be safely and conveniently pursued" (Keynes 1982 [1933], 239-41).

4

Trade and the Demand for Social Insurance

If increased international economic integration has constituted a key aspect of the postwar experience, a second striking feature has been the growth of government. Before World War II, the share of government expenditures in GDP averaged 21 percent in today's advanced industrial countries. By the mid-1990s, this figure had more than doubled to 47 percent (table 4.1). The increase in the role of government was particularly striking in countries such as the United States (from 9 to 34 percent), Sweden (from 10 to 69 percent), and the Netherlands (from 19 to 54 percent).

The increase in social spending, and income transfers in particular, drove the expansion of government in the postwar period. Figure 4.1 shows the record on such spending since 1960 for five member economies of the Organization for Economic Cooperation and Development (OECD): France, Germany, the United Kingdom, the United States, and Japan. In all five, spending on income transfers steadily increased until the early to mid-1980s and stabilized (or fell somewhat) thereafter. While most measures of government activity would show an increase over the postwar period, the rise in transfers stands out the most. This reflects the rise of the "welfare state," which many sociologists and political scientists consider "a key ingredient in the postwar consolidation of universal democracy" (Esping-Andersen 1994, 714).[1]

Economists have paid surprisingly little attention to the relationship between the growth of government and the intensification of international

---

1. See Lindert (1994) for a quantitative account of the evolution of social spending.

Table 4.1 Growth of government expenditure among industrial countries, 1870-1994 (percentage of GDP)

Country	Late 19th century (about 1870)	Pre-World War I (about 1913)	Post-World War I (about 1920)	Pre-World War II (about 1937)	Post-World War II (1960)	1980	1994
Austria	n.a.	n.a.	14.7	15.2	35.7	48.1	51.5
Belgium	n.a.	n.a.	n.a.	21.8	30.3	58.6	54.8
Canada	n.a.	n.a.	13.3	18.6	28.6	38.8	47.4
France	12.6	17.0	27.6	29.0	34.6	46.1	54.9
Germany	10.0	14.8	25.0	42.4	32.4	47.9	49.0
Italy	11.9	11.1	22.5	24.5	30.1	41.9	53.9
Japan	8.8	8.3	14.8	25.4	17.5	32.0	35.8
Netherlands	9.1	9.0	13.5	19.0	33.7	55.2	54.4
Norway	3.7	8.3	13.7	n.a.	29.9	37.5	55.6
Spain	n.a.	8.3	9.3	18.4	18.8	32.2	45.6
Sweden	5.7	6.3	8.1	10.4	31.0	60.1	68.8
Switzerland	n.a.	2.7	4.6	6.1	17.2	32.8	37.6
United Kingdom	9.4	12.7	26.2	30.0	32.2	43.0	42.9
United States	3.9	1.8	7.0	8.6	27.0	31.8	33.5
Average	8.3	9.1	15.4	20.7	28.5	43.3	49.0
Australia	n.a.	n.a.	n.a.	n.a.	21.2	31.6	37.5
Ireland	n.a.	n.a.	n.a.	n.a.	28.0	48.9	43.8
New Zealand	n.a.	n.a.	n.a.	n.a.	26.9	38.1	35.7
Average	n.a.	n.a.	n.a.	n.a.	25.4	39.5	39.0
Total average	8.3	9.1	15.4	20.7	27.9	42.6	47.2

n.a. = not available

Source: Tanzi and Schuknecht (1995).

economic integration. At first glance, the coexistence of these two trends appears spurious—a coincidence arising from the confluence of diverse determinants. For example, in a recent in-depth study Tanzi and Schuknecht (1995) attribute the expansion of government spending to determinants that are largely unrelated to the growth of trade: the Great Depression, changing beliefs about the economy and the efficacy of laissez-faire, the consequences of democratic populism, and interest-group pressures.

Political scientists, however, have read much more into the simultaneous expansion of trade *and* governments in the postwar period. Indeed, the relationship between dependence on trade and the scope of the government has been an ongoing preoccupation in the literature on comparative politics. Katzenstein (1985, 55), for example, has argued that it is no accident that small, highly open European economies such as Sweden, Austria, and the Netherlands have large governments. Governments in these economies have sought to provide a cushion against the risks of

Figure 4.1 Spending on social protection in five OECD countries, 1960-91 (as share of GDP)

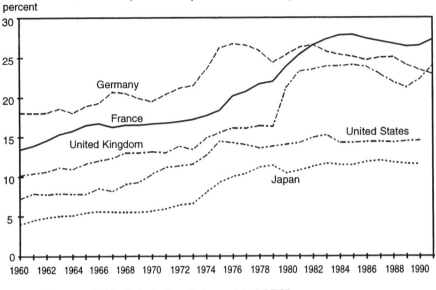

Source: Data supplied by Roberto Perotti, from original OECD sources.

exposure to international economic forces and have done so by extending their powers. As he notes (1985, 55):

> It was only in the 1950s and 1960s—that is, during the time of international liberalization—that the public sector assumed such a prominent role in the small European states. . . . In 1956-57 the share of social security expenditures in national income was identical, 13 percent in both the small European and the large industrial states; but by 1971 the small European states were on the average spending 20.9 percent of their GNP on social security compared to 14.3 percent for the large industrial states. . . . [T]he growth of public spending during the postwar years in "conservative" Switzerland exceeded the growth of spending in "socialist" Britain. [footnotes omitted]

Katzenstein (1984, 1985) has documented in detail how these small European states "complement[ed] their pursuit of liberalism in the international economy with a strategy of domestic compensation" (1985, 47)—entailing, among other policies, investment programs, incomes policies, industrial subsidies, and income transfers. Cameron (1978) and Garrett and Mitchell (1996) make similar arguments.

A closer look at the evidence indeed confirms that the relationship between openness to trade and the growth of government may not be a coincidence. Turning from time-series to cross-sectional evidence, for example, one uncovers a surprisingly robust positive association across

Figure 4.2 Relationship between openness and public expenditures in 23 OECD countries

government expenditures as percentage of GDP
(excluding interest), 1990-92

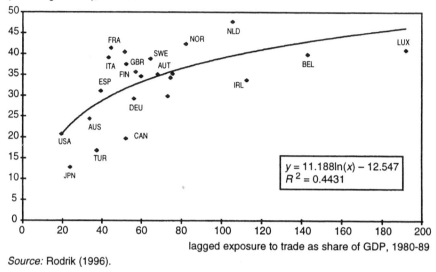

lagged exposure to trade as share of GDP, 1980-89

$$y = 11.188\ln(x) - 12.547$$
$$R^2 = 0.4431$$

Source: Rodrik (1996).

countries between the degree of exposure to international trade and the importance of the government in the economy. The point can be made with the help of two figures, reproduced from Rodrik (1996). Figure 4.2 shows the relationship between the share of government expenditures in GDP (excluding interest payments) and lagged exposure to trade (export plus imports divided by GDP) for 23 OECD countries during the early 1990s. The figure reveals an unmistakable positive association between openness and size of government. A semilogarithmic regression equation fits the data extremely well, explaining 44 percent of the cross-country variance in government expenditures. At one end of the distribution are the United States and Japan, which have the lowest trade shares in GDP and (along with Turkey and Canada) the lowest shares of government spending. At the other end are Luxembourg, Belgium, and the Netherlands, economies with very high degrees of openness and large governments.

Neither is the relationship confined to OECD economies. Figure 4.3 displays the *partial* correlation between openness and government consumption for 115 countries. I have controlled here for other potential determinants of government size, such as per capita income, demographic and economic structure, country size, and geography. The figure shows that there is a remarkably tight empirical association between openness to

Figure 4.3 Partial correlation between openness and government consumption in 115 countries (controlling for per capita income, urbanization, dependency ratio, area, and region)

log of government consumption as a percentage of GDP, 1985-89

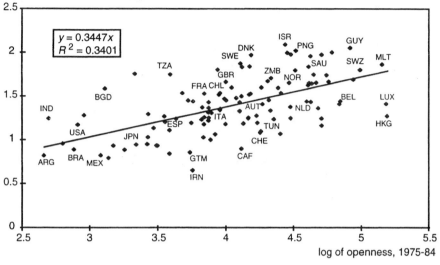

log of openness, 1975-84

trade and government consumption in this large cross-section of countries. Furthermore, exposure to trade in the early 1960s is a statistically significant predictor of the expansion in government size over the subsequent three decades in the same large sample of countries. These results turn out to be extremely robust. Further details are provided in Rodrik (1996).

What should we make of this? I will argue that the puzzle is solved by considering the importance of social insurance and the role of government in providing cover against external risk. Societies that expose themselves to greater amounts of external risk demand (and receive) a larger government role as shelter from the vicissitudes of global markets. In the context of the advanced industrial economies specifically, this translates into more generous social programs. Hence the conclusion that the social welfare state is the flip side of the open economy!

More evidence on this point is presented below. The main theme of this chapter is that globalization presents this dilemma: it results in increased demands on the state to provide social insurance while reducing the ability of the state to perform that role effectively. Consequently, as globalization proceeds, the social consensus required to maintain domestic markets open to international trade is endangered. With domestic political support for trade eroding, a return to old-style protectionism becomes a serious possibility.

The point that government policies lose their effectiveness in highly open economies should not be controversial. In particular, it is obvious that governments are constrained in raising taxes on footloose factors. When capital is perfectly mobile across national borders, for example, a domestic tax on capital is borne fully by immobile factors and not at all by capital itself.[2]

But if it is true, as argued above, that these immobile groups will demand more generous social programs as the price for accepting greater amounts of external risk, we have the makings of a serious conflict. In order to square the circle, governments have been forced to raise taxes on labor while reducing taxes on capital, as I will show later in the chapter.

Because some of these ideas may strike the reader as fanciful, or at least unsubstantiated, this chapter will focus on the empirical evidence. I will present three types. First, I will use cross-country evidence from a broad sample of countries to show that external risk does matter: the greater the exposure to external risk, the greater the aggregate income and consumption risk to which domestic residents are subjected.

Second, drawing a distinction between *openness* and *exposure to external risk*, I will show that higher levels of government spending (as a share of GDP) are associated with greater exposure to external risk and that, once external risk is explicitly controlled for, governments in more open economies do not spend more. Hence the positive correlation between openness and size of government discussed above seems to have exposure to external risk as its root cause.

Third, I will use panel evidence on different types of government spending and of taxes for the advanced industrial countries since the 1960s. With panel data, I cannot separately control for external risk because my risk variable uses data on terms-of-trade variability over a two-decade period. But the panel approach has the advantage of providing information about how government activity has responded to *changes* in international economic integration in each country, holding constant the risk characteristics of each country's trade (the latter being absorbed into the fixed effects).[3] Thus, controlling for country and year effects, I find that increases in openness have resulted in *reductions* in social spending and

---

2. This is, of course, one reason for the movement toward "unitary" taxation—that is, the taxation of foreign-owned firms on the basis of their global income. Some have argued that by appropriately designing the tax regime (and effectively taxing "old" capital but not "new") a government can continue to collect substantial revenue from capitalists despite open borders (see, e.g., Wallerstein and Przeworski 1995). I do not find such arguments very persuasive. Aside from the problem of time inconsistency—there is always the temptation to redefine old capital—it is not clear that the Wallerstein-Przeworski proposal would raise adequate revenue in the long run.

3. Fixed effects control for country-specific variables that are not otherwise included as regressors in the regressions.

government consumption. This depressing effect on spending is larger in countries with no restrictions on capital mobility. Further, I will present evidence that the distribution of the tax burden has shifted from capital to labor as integration has advanced: as openness increases, taxes on capital decrease while taxes on labor income increase.

I use a formal model in appendix A to sharpen the argument. The model highlights several things. First, the ability of the owners of capital to move in and out of the domestic economy with relative ease imposes a negative externality on other groups (such as labor) with more limited mobility. This externality arises because capital mobility exacerbates the risks to which immobile groups are exposed. Second, the model shows that a strategy of compensating internationally immobile groups for accepting greater amounts of external risk can work as long as international economic integration is not too advanced. But once globalization moves beyond a certain point, the government can no longer finance the requisite income transfers because the tax base becomes too footloose. Hence at high levels of integration there is a serious conflict between openness and maintaining social consensus.

Is External Risk Important?

I begin by using cross-country evidence from a broad sample of countries to show that exposure to external risk does increase aggregate income and consumption risk. It is not obvious that this should be the case, so the evidence on this point is important. It is entirely possible, on theoretical grounds, that external risk would counteract exposure to *domestic* sources of risk, nullifying the hypothesis of a trade-off between openness and stability. This could happen for a couple of reasons. First, increased international integration of capital markets may allow all domestic residents, including workers, to diversify internationally, reducing consumption risk. Second, world markets being larger than domestic markets, the effects of idiosyncratic, country-specific shocks may be felt less in economies more tightly integrated with world markets.

On the other hand, specialization according to comparative advantage can be expected to result in more concentrated production structures and. hence in greater income variability. In addition, a significant part of workers' income is embodied in human capital, which in practice is impossible to diversify even under full capital mobility. Hence it is ultimately an empirical question whether increased exposure to risk of external origin is associated with increased exposure to risk in the aggregate.

Table 4.2 provides rather strong evidence that the answer is affirmative. This table shows the results of regressing indicators of aggregate risk on a measure of external risk across a sample of 105 countries for which the requisite data were available. The measure of external risk I have selected

Table 4.2 Impact of external risk on volatility of income and consumption

Independent variable	Dependent variable (standard deviation of growth rates of)[a]			
	Real GDP adjusted for terms of trade	Real GDP	Real "private" GDP	Real consumption
Constant	0.026* (0.003)	0.026* (0.003)	0.025* (0.003)	0.027* (0.004)
Real per capita income, 1975	−4.22E-07 (3.97E-07)	−3.40E-07 (3.64E-07)	−1.42E-07 (3.91E-07)	−7.53E-07 (7.37E-07)
Socialist countries	0.001 (0.006)	0.001 (0.005)	0.004 (0.006)	0.006 (0.005)
OECD	−0.012* (0.004)	−0.012* (0.004)	−0.013* (0.004)	−0.013*** (0.007)
Latin America	−0.006 (0.004)	−0.005 (0.004)	−0.005 (0.003)	−0.005 (0.004)
East Asia	−0.012* (0.003)	−0.011* (0.003)	−0.011* (0.003)	−0.016* (0.006)
Sub-Saharan Africa	0.001 (0.004)	0.002 (0.004)	0.004 (0.004)	0.006 (0.004)
Exposure to external risk (OPENAVG6092 × TOTDLOGSTD)	0.0007* (0.0002)	0.0004** (0.0002)	0.0006* (0.0002)	0.0012* (0.0003)
Number of observations	104	104	104	104
Adjusted R²	0.39	0.36	0.36	0.48

* = 99% significance; ** = 95% significance; *** = 90% significance.

a. Standard errors in parentheses.

is the one suggested by theory, namely the volatility of the streams of income associated with fluctuations in the external terms of trade. This is calculated as the product of openness ($[x + m]/y$) and the standard deviation of the first logarithmic differences in the terms of trade (with the variable name TOTDLOGSTD).[4] Using an alternative measure of exter-

---

4. Formally, let x, m, and y stand for volumes of exports, imports, and GDP, respectively. Let π be the natural logarithm of the price of exports relative to imports (the terms of trade). Let the log of the terms of trade follow a random walk, possibly with drift (a hypothesis that cannot be rejected for most countries). The unanticipated component of the income

nal risk, based on the product concentration of exports, yields very similar results (results for this second measure are not shown here).

The dependent variables are four measures of income or consumption risk, calculated as the standard deviation of the first log differences in real GDP adjusted for the terms of trade, real GDP, real GDP excluding government consumption (denoted as private GDP), and real consumption. Additional dependent variables are per capita income and a range of country-grouping and regional dummies.

The results show that the three measures of income risk, as well as consumption risk, increase with exposure to external risk. This finding is robust to the inclusion of a wide range of additional controls and holds equally well when the sample is restricted to the high-income countries.[5] Note in particular that the estimated coefficient on external risk is largest in the regression on *consumption* risk, which is notable because one might have expected capital mobility to allow diversification of consumption risk (even if income risk cannot be diversified away).

To get a sense of the magnitudes involved, consider the estimated effect on consumption risk of an increase in external risk by one standard deviation. The standard deviation of the external risk variable is 5.6 (which corresponds to a standard deviation in the growth rates of external income of $\frac{1}{2} \times 5.6 = 2.8$ percent). According to the last column in table 4.2, this would be associated with an increase in the standard deviation of consumption growth of $5.6 \times 0.0012 = 0.67$ percent. The median value of the standard deviation of consumption growth in the sample is 2.63 percent. Hence the implied effect is not negligible.

Note further that these aggregate relationships say nothing about the *distribution* of risk within the economy. Presumably, this kind of risk is borne disproportionately by groups with low international mobility. Once its incidence is taken into account, therefore, the problem of external risk is likely to loom larger.

Cross-Country Evidence on Openness, External Risk, and Government Activity

I now turn to a more direct look at the consequences of external risk for government behavior. The evidence presented earlier showed that there is

---

effects of a terms-of-trade change can then be expressed (as a percentage of GDP) as $\frac{1}{2}[(x + m)/y][d\pi - \alpha]$, where α is the trend growth rate in the terms of trade. The standard deviation of this is $\frac{1}{2}[(x + m)/y] \times$ standard deviation of $d\pi$.

5. It is also robust to instrumenting for openness, OPENAVG6092 (which in principle is an endogenous variable), by using a set of exogenous geographical and country-size variables (results not shown).

a close association between exposure to trade and the scale of government spending in a broad cross-section of countries. A more systematic look at the evidence suggests that the reason has to do with external risk: exposure to external risk has resulted in demands for a more active government role in the provision of social insurance.

Working with data from a cross-section of countries, it is possible to distinguish empirically between *exposure to external risk* and *openness*, as in the previous section. Intuitively, two economies can be equally exposed to trade yet have quite different levels of exposure to external risk if their terms of trade differ in their volatility. For example, the ratio of trade to GDP is around 20 percent in both Japan and the United States, yet the terms of trade are almost twice as volatile in Japan. New Zealand and the United Kingdom are equally open (around 55 percent), but New Zealand's terms of trade fluctuate twice as much as the United Kingdom's. Note also that the empirical measure of openness used here (total trade divided by GDP) is only a rough proxy for the theoretically relevant measure—the sensitivity of the domestic economy to events on the other side of the border. Imperfect as it is, this measure should capture to some extent the maneuvering room that domestic agents—private and public—have.

In this exercise, both openness and exposure to external risk are entered in the regressions as independent variables explaining the magnitude of government spending. We can then see whether openness is still positively related to government spending once external risk is controlled for.

I use two measures of government spending. One is social security and welfare spending—which includes unemployment compensation, family assistance, and pensions—averaged over 1985-89. Old-age insurance is typically the largest item in social security and welfare spending in the advanced industrial countries. Such insurance is obviously not targeted on dislocations arising specifically from trade. But it does reduce lifetime uncertainty over incomes, and as such it contributes to a greater sense of security, irrespective of the source of the shocks to which incomes are subject. So one would expect to find a positive correlation between exposure to external risk and social security and welfare spending.

The second measure is government consumption (which excludes income transfers as well as public investment), also averaged over 1985-89. This measure has the advantage that it is available for over 100 countries on a standardized basis (thanks to Penn World Tables 1995). Its disadvantage is that the links between government spending on such things as education and the military and the provision of social insurance are more tenuous. Nonetheless, in lower-income countries, where social security and welfare systems are difficult to set up, the evidence suggests that government purchases of goods and services do indeed perform an insurance function.

Table 4.3 Effect of openness and external risk on log of government expenditures as share of GDP by income group and type
(averaged over 1985-89)

Independent variable	OECD countries		Countries with 1985 per capita GDP > $4,500		All countries[a]	
	Social security and welfare	Government consumption	Social security and welfare	Government consumption	Social security and welfare	Government consumption
Openness (OPENAVG7584)	−0.170*	−0.005	−0.043***	−0.006***	−0.018	−0.004***
Instability in terms of trade (TOTDLOGSTD)	−134.088*	−8.329	−35.010**	−4.148***	−16.484*	−3.585*
Exposure to external risk (OPENAVG7584 × TOTDLOGSTD)	1.869*	0.070	0.438**	0.067**	0.183***	0.056*
Number of observations	19	22	25	32	68	109
Adjusted R²	0.75	0.18	0.23	0.09	0.48	0.51

* = 99% significance; ** = 95% significance; *** = 90% significance.

a. Regressions in last two columns include the following other regressors: log(GDPSH585), log(DEPEND90), log(URBAN90), SOC, OECD, LAAM, ASIAE, and SAFRICA. Coefficients on these additional regressors are not shown. See appendix for variable definitions.

The first two columns of table 4.3 focus on the OECD countries. The results with social security and welfare spending strongly support the argument. As expected, exposure to external risk is positively correlated with social security and welfare spending (at the 99 percent confidence level). The coefficient on openness here turns negative (and is also statistically significant). Terms-of-trade volatility, which is entered independently in these regressions, also has a negative and significant estimated coefficient. Taken together, these results suggest that income transfers tend to be largest in economies that are simultaneously very open *and* subject to substantial price risk in world markets. While the sample is small (19), these variables together account for 75 percent of the variation in social security and welfare spending across these countries. By contrast, in this OECD sample, openness and external risk indicators have no explanatory power for spending on government consumption.

The next two columns enlarge the sample to all countries with 1985 GDP per capita above $4,500. The results with regard to social security and welfare spending are qualitatively the same, although the estimated coefficients are much smaller and the levels of statistical significance lower. The main change now is that the openness and risk variables begin to enter significantly in the regression on government consumption as well, although the overall fit is still not impressive.

The last two columns display results for all countries for which the requisite data are available. These regressions also include additional controls for per capita income, economic structure, demography, and geographic region. The pattern of signs is once again in accord with the expectation, and the estimated coefficients are mostly significant. But note that the variables of interest now do much worse in the regression on social security and welfare spending than they do in the one on government consumption. I attribute this to the fact that social security and welfare spending is largely a mixed bag in lower-income countries, and that most such countries do not have the capacity to run adequate welfare systems. It is plausible that some of the same insurance functions are provided in these countries through government employment and government purchases of goods and services (as captured in government consumption). The regression results displayed in the last column of the table strongly support this hypothesis. See Rodrik (1996) for more evidence on this score.[6]

To summarize, the cross-country evidence provides strong support for the ideas discussed above. Government spending—on social security and welfare in the rich countries and consumption in poorer countries—is highest in countries that are exposed to significant amounts of external risk. Since exposure to external risk is the consequence both of high levels of trade and of volatility in the prices of traded goods, it is the interaction of these two that seems to matter. Holding either one of these constant while varying the other has an ambiguous effect on government spending.

Evidence from Panel Data for the OECD Countries

Cross-country evidence has a number of shortcomings. In particular, drawing inferences from such evidence about the consequences of changes in openness or external risk for any given country is problematic except under very restrictive assumptions. Hence it would be useful to have

6. Several readers have wondered whether these results may be due to the negative correlation between country size and exposure to trade: larger countries tend to have smaller trade in relation to GDP, and in the presence of scale economies in the provision of public services, we will observe a negative relationship between size and the government share. The answer is that there does not seem to be such a bias. The results discussed here are robust to the inclusion of explicit measures of country size—such as population, total GDP, and land area—on the right-hand side of the regressions (Rodrik 1996).

supplementary evidence drawn from combined cross-country, time-series data using panel techniques. I present this kind of evidence here for the advanced industrial countries for which annual data on social spending and tax rates are available beginning in the mid-1960s.[7] The countries included are most of the OECD members, including Australia, Austria, Canada, Denmark, Finland, France, Germany, Italy, Japan, Netherlands, Norway, Sweden, the United Kingdom, and the United States.

This approach, however, has a problem of its own. Because the external risk variable is constructed using terms-of-trade data over the 1971-90 period, it is not possible to obtain a time-varying measure of external risk that is independent from openness. Therefore, unlike in the previous section, I cannot test to see whether government spending reacts differently to openness and external risk. Terms-of-trade volatility will now be absorbed into the fixed effects for each country. But I can examine how government spending on income transfers (as well as government consumption) has reacted to changes in openness, *after country and year effects are controlled for.*[8]

The results are displayed in table 4.4 for two types of government expenditures: spending that is classified by the OECD as "spending on social protection," which includes income transfers, and government consumption. Both are expressed as percentages of GDP. The explanatory variables include (lagged) openness and GDP per capita, as well as a full set of country and year dummies (coefficients for the latter are not separately shown). I find a negative relationship between income per capita and government spending of both types, which goes against Wagner's law.[9] More relevant for my purposes, I find that social spending and government consumption both respond negatively to lagged increases in openness. The estimated coefficients suggest that an increase in the shares of imports plus exports in GDP of 5 percentage points (which translates into an increase in the measure of openness of 10 percentage points) results in a reduction in social spending of about 0.3 percentage points.

The table also adds as regressors dummy variables for the presence of restrictions on capital mobility, both individually and in interaction with

---

7. The data used in this section were made available by Roberto Perotti (spending on social protection) and Gian Maria Milesi-Ferretti (taxes), to whom I am grateful. The original source for the spending data is the OECD.

8. Alternatively, one could try to construct a time-varying estimate of external risk by using terms-of-trade data for shorter subsamples (e.g., using five-year windows). However, the value added from this approach is not quite clear. In the current framework, it is reasonable to suppose that the "riskiness" of each country's trade is absorbed into the fixed effect. The panel regressions reported in this section have also been estimated using a random-effects model. The results were essentially identical and so are not presented here.

9. Wagner's law states that the demand for public services is income-elastic, so that the share of government spending in national income increases as incomes rise.

Table 4.4 Relationship between government spending (as percentage of GDP) and openness in OECD countries, 1966-91[a]

Independent variable	Social spending	Government consumption	Social spending	Government consumption
Openness (lagged)	−0.028*** (0.015)	−0.029* (0.013)	−0.064* (0.018)	−0.053* (0.013)
GDP per capita	−0.001* (0.000)	−0.001* (0.000)	−0.001* (0.000)	−0.001* (0.000)
Openness (lagged) × capital account restrictions			0.030** (0.012)	0.021* (0.006)
Capital account restrictions			−0.041 (0.730)	−0.023 (0.353)
F	56.47	10.31	47.85	13.10
Prob > F	0.000	0.000	0.000	0.000
Number of observations	502	571	426	456
R^2	0.77	0.35	0.77	0.46

* = 99% significance; ** = 95% significance; *** = 90% significance.

a. Data are annual. Estimated using fixed effects. Year dummies included (coefficients not shown). Standard errors are in parentheses.

openness.[10] The results are interesting in that they show the negative effect of openness on spending to be particularly strong in countries or periods without restrictions on capital mobility. Hence the magnitude of the effect discussed in the previous paragraph is more than doubled in cases where the capital account is entirely free.

How do we relate the results of this section to those of the previous one? They are less conflicting than might at first appear. The question that we are now asking is this: what is the relationship between openness and government spending, holding the volatility of the terms-of-trade constant? The cross-country evidence suggested that the answer is ambiguous because there are offsetting effects to consider. For any given terms-

---

10. The source for the dummy variables are the summary table in the International Monetary Fund's annual reports on exchange arrangements and exchange restrictions. I am grateful to Andy Rose for making this data set available to me in electronic form.

of-trade risk, an increase in openness increases the demand for social insurance, but it also reduces the ability to finance the requisite spending. Which effect dominates empirically depends on the precise level at which the terms-of-trade volatility is being held constant. For a set of countries with high levels of terms-of-trade volatility, the cross-country results suggest that increased openness will be associated with expanded spending. For countries with low levels of terms-of-trade volatility, on the other hand, such as the OECD countries, the reverse will be true, and increased openness will be associated with reduced government spending. That is indeed what the findings suggest.[11]

The bottom line, therefore, is that increased openness since the mid-1960s has been associated with reductions in government activity in the advanced industrial countries. Hence while countries that are exposed to significant amounts of external risk traditionally have had governments playing a more substantial role in the provision of social insurance, it becomes increasingly difficult to discharge this role as economic integration advances.

The manner in which the dilemma has been resolved on the revenue side is quite interesting (table 4.5). This table shows results from panel regressions similar to those above, except that the dependent variables are now tax rates on labor and capital income, respectively. These tax rates have been estimated from national income accounts by Mendoza, Milesi-Ferretti, and Asea (1996), using a methodology developed by Mendoza, Razin, and Tesar (1994). They are available for 1965-91 for 18 OECD countries.[12] The table shows that taxes on labor respond positively to increases in lagged openness, while taxes on capital respond negatively: the estimated coefficient on openness is positive and statistically significant in the regression on labor taxes, while it is negative and statistically significant in the regression on capital taxes. In other words, there is strong evidence that as economic integration advances the tax burden of social insurance programs is shifted from capital to labor.

More visual evidence is displayed in figure 4.4, which shows the unweighted average of tax rates on capital and labor in four leading industrial countries: France, Germany, the United Kingdom, and the

---

11. For example, the first column of table 4.3 shows the change in social spending as openness increases, which is given by $-0.170 + (1.869 \times \text{TOTDLOGSTD})$. For levels of TOTDLOGSTD less than $0.170/1.869 = 0.091$, the relationship is negative. The median value of TOTDLOGSTD for the OECD sample is just above this threshold, at 0.092. This assumes, of course, that the cross-country and time-series evidence can be directly compared in this manner. An alternative perspective is that the cross-country evidence reflects some long-run tendencies while the panel evidence is more germane to short-term adjustments.

12. These are Australia, Austria, Belgium, Canada, Denmark, Finland, France, Germany, Italy, Japan, the Netherlands, New Zealand, Norway, Spain, Sweden, Switzerland, the United Kingdom, and the United States.

Table 4.5 Relationship between taxes and openness in OECD countries, 1965-92[a]

Independent variable	Tax rate on labor income	Tax rate on capital income	Tax rate on labor income	Tax rate on capital income
Openness (lagged)	0.108* (0.019)	−0.122** (0.051)	0.069* (0.021)	−0.082 (0.051)
GDP per capita	0.000 (0.000)	−0.000 (0.001)	−0.000 (0.000)	−0.000 (0.001)
Openness (lagged) × capital account restrictions			0.061* (0.020)	0.256* (0.052)
Capital account restrictions			−1.135 (0.925)	−14.330* (2.394)
F	45.61	8.43	41.35	8.72
Prob > F	0.000	0.000	0.000	0.000
Number of observations	371	371	343	343
R^2	0.80	0.42	0.80	0.46

* = 99% significance; ** = 95% significance.

a. Data are annual. Estimated using fixed effects. Year dummies included (coefficients not shown). Standard errors are in parentheses.

United States. The two trends exhibit a clear turning point in the early 1980s. Since the early 1980s, taxes on capital have come down sharply, while taxes on labor have kept increasing at the same rate as before.

Hence the evidence suggests three things: globalization reduces the ability of governments to spend resources on social programs, it makes it more difficult to tax capital, and labor now carries a growing share of the tax burden.

Recapitulation

It is generally accepted that integration into the world economy reduces the ability of governments to undertake redistributive taxation or implement generous social programs. The evidence discussed above reinforces this presumption. It is less well understood that this may create a serious dilemma where maintaining political support for open markets is con-

Figure 4.4 France, Germany, United States, and United Kingdom: taxes on labor and capital, 1970-91

unweighted averages

cerned. This chapter provided concrete evidence on that score as well. In particular, it has shown that societies (rich and poor alike) have demanded and received a larger government role as the price of exposing themselves to greater amounts of external risk.[13] I read this evidence as pointing to a tension between the consequences of globalization and the requirements of maintaining the social legitimacy of free trade.

The postwar economic order was based on a bargain that John Ruggie has termed "the compromise of embedded liberalism":

> Societies were asked to embrace the change and dislocation attending international liberalization. In turn, liberalization and its effects were cushioned by the newly acquired domestic economic and social policy roles of governments. (Ruggie 1995, 508)

By any standard, this bargain has served the world economy extremely well. Spurred by liberalization, world trade has expanded phenomenally since the 1950s without causing major social dislocations or generating much opposition in the advanced industrial countries.

Despite the perception of a backlash against the welfare state, the principles behind the welfare state remain highly popular among broad seg-

---

13. This argument parallels the view expressed by Sinn (1995, 1996) that the social-welfare state is an insurance mechanism that makes lifetime careers safer and hence encourages beneficial risk taking.

Table 4.6 Public support for social programs (percent favoring)

Program	United Kingdom	United States	Australia	West Germany	Austria	Italy
More spending on health care						
Poorest quartile	90	66	69	54	73	82
Wealthiest quartile	84	54	55	33	59	78
More spending on pensions						
Poorest quartile	87	60	63	51	61	79
Wealthiest quartile	63	37	45	32	50	75
More spending on unemployment benefits						
Poorest quartile	59	47	19	41	27	63
Wealthiest quartile	25	14	7	19	13	52
Government reduction of income differences between those with high and low incomes						
Poorest quartile	58	49	51	63	70	79
Wealthiest quartile	37	22	30	52	62	64

Source: Taylor-Gooby (1989).

ments of society. In the United Kingdom, for example, where the conservative revolution perhaps has gone furthest, one review of opinion polls concludes: "There has been no strong shift against the welfare state. To the contrary the main services are as strongly supported as they have been at any time since the war" (Taylor-Gooby 1985, 51). In the United States, Social Security, Medicare, and unemployment insurance also remain very popular. The share of respondents who reject cuts in Social Security to balance the budget is consistently above 80 percent.[14] A cross-national survey carried out in 1985 at the height of the conservative revolution (summarized in table 4.6) reveals substantial popular support in much of Europe and the United States for expanded spending on social programs. As expected, however, there are also some important class differences in preferences for social spending, particularly in the Anglo-Saxon countries (United States, Britain, and Australia).

---

14. One could even argue that the 1980s experienced a shift in US public opinion toward a more positive feeling about the size and power of government. Writing in the conservative journal *The Public Interest* in 1992, Mayer says: "Not only is public opinion today more supportive of domestic spending, it is also less responsive to such conservative themes as taxes and big government" (1992, 15).

But can the bargain of "embedded liberalism" be sustained? It is questionable that it can if governments lose their autonomy in generating tax revenues and shaping social policies. In the words of Ruggie again (1994, 2), a "source of potentially serious problems for the international trade regime [is] the growing inability of governments at home to sustain their part of the social compact on which postwar international liberalization has hinged." The fact that confidence in government has declined in most advanced industrial countries (Nye 1996) while support for its welfare functions remain high is indicative of this tension.

I do not mean to suggest that the government is the sole provider of social insurance in modern economies, nor do I imply that such insurance is best provided at the level of national governments. There are mediating institutions, such as local governments, religious organizations, private charities, and the extended family, that play the same role. Many of these, of course, have come under the same kind of pressures under the force of globalization as have national governments. In the future, perhaps social insurance will devolve more to these other institutions and to others that are not yet playing this role. What seems clear is that we need some creative thinking on how to provide social insurance and thereby foster stability in the new global economy.

5

Implications

If the arguments this book makes are right, there are two dangers arising from complacency toward the social consequences of globalization. The first of these, and the more obvious, is a political backlash against trade. The candidacy of Patrick Buchanan in the Republican primaries of the 1996 presidential election revealed that protectionism can be a rather easy sell when broad segments of American society are experiencing anxieties linked, at least in part, to globalization. One wonders how much greater Buchanan's support would have been had the unemployment rate been, say, 10 percent rather than 5.6 percent. Economists may complain that protectionism is mere snake oil and argue that the ailments require altogether different medicine. But intellectual arguments will not win hearts and minds unless there are concrete solutions on offer. Trade protection, for all its faults, has the benefit of concreteness.

Perhaps future Buchanans will be ultimately defeated, as Buchanan himself was, by the common sense of the public. Even so, there is a second and perhaps even more serious danger: that globalization will contribute to social disintegration, as nations are split along lines of economic status, mobility, region, or social norms. Even without a protectionist backlash, a victory for globalization that comes at the price of social disintegration will be a very hollow victory indeed.

Social Disintegration as the Price of Economic Integration?

If not handled well, then, the social pressures unleashed by global economic integration will likely result in bad economics *and* bad governance.

This is not only because globalization highlights and exacerbates tensions among groups, which it does. It is also because it reduces the willingness of internationally mobile groups to cooperate with others in resolving disagreements and conflicts.

Far-sighted companies will tend to their own communities as they globalize. But an employer that has an "exit" option is one that is less likely to exercise the "voice" option. It is so much easier to outsource than to enter a debate on how to revitalize the local economy. This means that owners of internationally mobile factors become disengaged from their local communities and disinterested in their development and prosperity—just as suburban flight in an earlier era condemned many urban areas to neglect.

"[D]iverse groups [in society] hold together," wrote Bernard Crick (1962, 24), "because they practice politics—not because they agree about 'fundamentals,' or some such concept too vague, too personal, or too divine ever to do the job of politics for it. The moral consensus of a free state is not something mysteriously prior to or above politics: it is the activity (the civilizing activity) of politics itself." Or as Albert Hirschman (1994, 25) put it, "The community spirit that is normally needed in a democratic market society tends to be spontaneously generated through the experience of tending the conflicts that are typical of that society." But what if globalization reduces the incentives to "tend" to these conflicts? What if, by reducing the civic engagement of internationally mobile groups, globalization loosens the civic glue that holds societies together and exacerbates social fragmentation?[1]

Hence globalization delivers a double blow to social cohesion—first by exacerbating conflict over fundamental beliefs regarding social organization and second by weakening the forces that would normally militate for the resolution of these conflicts through national debate and deliberation.

These developments are afflicting all societies exposed to globalization, with many developing countries perhaps even more exposed than the advanced industrial countries. A recent analysis of Mexican society by Jorge Castañeda (1996) is worth quoting extensively. Castañeda speaks of "a new cleavage that is rapidly cutting across Mexican society":

> This split separates those Mexicans plugged into the US economy from those who are not. . . . It divides Mexicans who are highly sensitive to government

---

1. Here the debate on globalization joins the debate on social capital (Putnam 1996). Putnam documents a significant decline in civic participation in the United States, and attributes it, in large part, to television. There is now considerable empirical evidence that suggests social fragmentation is detrimental to economic performance. Alesina and Rodrik (1994), among others, show that income inequality reduces subsequent economic growth, Knack and Keefer (1996) find levels of social trust to be positively correlated with investment, and Easterly and Levine (1996) find a strong negative correlation between an index of ethnolinguistic fragmentation and subsequent levels of economic growth.

macroeconomic policy from those who are indifferent to it. It separates those who correctly believe that politics and events in Mexico still determine their destiny from those who just as rightly understand that the decisions most critical to their lives are made in Washington and New York. It parts Mexicans who remain on the margins of global flows of capital, goods, and services, even if they are not on the margins of Mexican society, from those who are steadily being integrated into those flows. This growing group of Mexicans oriented toward the United States is isolated from much of the country's economic tribulation and relatively complacent about its political travails. (95)

With between one-fifth and one-quarter of the Mexican population tied into the world economy in this fashion, Castañeda doubts that a social explosion will happen. But, as he emphasizes, the presence of this group also makes meaningful reform less likely: "[W]ithout a stake in political change, [the segments of Mexican society linked to the world economy] also have little reason to foster it" (1996, 100). Castañeda's account vividly describes an extreme form of the syndromes associated with globalization *cum* social disintegration.

Markets are a social institution, and their continued existence is predicated on the perception that their processes and outcomes are legitimate. As Karl Polanyi (1944) pointed out more than 50 years ago, the international market is the only market that is not regulated by an overarching political authority. Consequently, transactions undertaken in the international marketplace carry the least inherent legitimacy. This in itself is an ongoing source of tension between globalization and society. The problem becomes much worse when segments of society are perceived as having broken their links with their local communities and become footloose. Institutions that lose their legitimacy can no longer function, and markets are no different.

As John Ruggie put it (1995, 508), "In some respects . . . the world [today] finds itself faced with a challenge which is not unlike the one it faced in 1945: devising compatible forms of international liberalization and domestic stability." That challenge is augmented by some key difficulties. The United States is neither willing nor able to play the kind of leadership role it did in the immediate aftermath of World War II, and there is no alternative leader. Perhaps more seriously, there is a lack of clear strategies on which to proceed, even if the United States or another country were to provide the leadership.

Policy Implications

As emphasized in the introductory chapter, many of the underlying changes that have occurred in the global economy are now irreversible. Advances in transportation and communications technologies render national borders more porous to foreign competition than they have ever been, and nothing short of drastic government restrictions can alter that. Protectionism is not a solution because it would likely generate its own set of social conflicts, even if one were to discount its costs in terms of economic efficiency. There are no easy fixes. We need to think imaginatively and creatively, without being blinded by ideologies that lead us to overlook problems and/or their potential solutions.

John Maynard Keynes, one of the architects of the postwar international economic system, once argued that the lack of intelligent alternatives to free trade and economic liberalism was a key obstacle to implementing a more desirable social system. "It must be admitted," he wrote, "that [the principles of laissez-faire] have been confirmed in the minds of sound thinkers and reasonable public by the poor quality of the opponent proposals—protectionism on the one hand, and Marxian socialism on the other" (Keynes 1972 [1926], 285). Keynes, of course, was hardly an unadulterated free trader.[2] What we need today is the same kind of pragmatic approach to public policy problems that Keynes offered in his own time.

The Role of Economists

There is a big role in this for economists. International economists in particular have been too Panglossian about the consequences of globalization. Their approach on the labor-market consequences of trade, one area in which they have actually engaged in the debate, has been too narrow, resulting in a tendency to downplay the role of trade. They have been too quick to paint those who have taken a more concerned stance as ignorant of economics or as closet protectionists (and sometimes both). Largely as a consequence, they have shut themselves out of the broader policy debate. This is a pity because economics has much to contribute here.

For example, there is much thinking to do on how to design appropriate policies and institutions that can best address the need to provide social insurance, which I have argued is a critical complement to the expansion of global markets. As a general principle, the better targeted the policies

---

2. In particular, he saw a potential role for import tariffs—for, well, Keynesian reasons having to do with aggregate demand and employment. In an oft-quoted article entitled "National Self-Sufficiency" (published in 1933), he went so far as to argue that international economic relations among nations could be a source of international conflict. Hence the famous passage: "I sympathise, therefore, with those who would minimise, rather than those who would maximise, economic entanglement between nations. Ideas, knowledge, art, hospitality, travel—these are things which should of their nature be international. But let goods be homespun whenever it is reasonable and conveniently possible; and, above all, let finance be primarily national." The rest of the paragraph is not quoted as often: "Yet, at the same time, those who seek to disembarrass a country from its entanglements should be slow and wary. It should not be a matter of tearing up roots but of slowly training a plant to grow a different direction" (Keynes 1982 [1933], 236).

are to the sources of the problem, the less cost they will entail. If the external risks that buffet national economies and workers were fully observable, a set of transfers contingent on the realization of the shocks would work best. But the world is obviously too complicated for first-best solutions, and realistically we will have to sacrifice some efficiency. So economists can help develop practical alternatives that provide some insulation for the most affected groups without blunting market incentives entirely. It is not entirely clear what role trade policy should play in this, if any at all.[3]

Similarly, the mobility of capital and of employers both aggravate the risks immobile groups face and render it more difficult to generate the public resources needed to finance social insurance schemes. If this results in globalization coming up against social and political constraints and a backlash against trade, the mobility of employers creates a worldwide negative externality. A logical implication is that some taxation of foot-loose factors at the global level, with revenue sharing among nations, may be worth considering. There is a parallel here with the ongoing discussion of the Tobin tax, with the difference that the current idea applies to physical (rather than financial) capital. Once again, there is much thinking to do about the rationale and design of such a policy.

Finally, economists can draw on the literatures on institutional economics and political economy to formulate designs for a new system of global safeguards. As I will argue further below, addressing the concerns discussed here will likely require a mixture of greater multilateral discipline and broader access to an escape clause. The challenge is to enable countries that are willing to engage in greater harmonization of domestic policies to do so, while also allowing them to selectively delink from international obligations when these obligations come into conflict with domestic norms or institutions. How best to achieve this is an exciting intellectual challenge, with potentially large practical payoffs. I will discuss my own ideas on this later in this chapter.

Hence economists could play a much more constructive role if they were to recognize that the tensions between social stability and globalization are real. They could help develop the conceptual frameworks needed for rethinking the roles of governments and of international institutions in this new phase of the global economy. They could assist policymakers in finding the tools and instruments needed to achieve policy objectives rather than taking issue with the objectives or denying that the problems exist.

By becoming engaged in this broader debate, economists can establish greater credibility with the public as they attempt to clear up the misunder-

---

3. As expressed by Avinash Dixit in his comments on an earlier draft, "Designing more efficient systems of social insurance, tailored to the particular shocks that matter to particular countries, which will allow them to secure more of the benefits of integration and suffer less of the social costs of it, is just the right kind of task for economists."

standings that opponents of trade often propagate. Keeping the debate honest and grounded on solid empirical evidence is a natural role for economists.

William Greider's recent book, *One World, Ready or Not—The Manic Logic of Global Capitalism* (1997), illustrates the appeal of many popular misconceptions for some commentators. One of the main themes of Greider's book—that the global expansion of markets is undermining social cohesion and moving the world inexorably toward a major economic and political crisis—might be viewed simply as a bolder expression of the potential danger I have highlighted here. Certainly, I am in sympathy with many of Greider's concerns—the consequences for low-skilled workers in the advanced industrial countries, the weakening of social safety nets, and the repression of political rights in some leading exporters such as China and Indonesia. However, the book's disregard for sound economic analysis and for systematic empirical evidence makes it a very unreliable treatise on what is happening and a faulty manual for setting things right.

The misconceptions that crop up in Greider's book are easy ones for economists to correct. Greider is wrong, for example, in thinking that low wages are the driving force behind today's global commerce. If that were so, the world's most formidable exporters would be Bangladesh and a smattering of African countries. What he fails to take into account is the importance of differences among countries in labor productivity. Furthermore, Greider (1997, 205) is wrong to attribute the US trade deficit to the "unbalanced behavior" of US trade partners. If commercial policies determined trade imbalances, India, until recently one of the world's most protectionist countries, would have been running large trade surpluses. It is a mistake to claim that "the global economy [is] now a losing transaction for the nation as a whole" because the United States' net factor payments abroad are positive (202). It is far from true that outward-oriented industrialization in Southeast Asian countries has made life worse rather than better for the former farmers who now toil in factories. It is generally not the case that foreign-owned companies in developing countries provide inferior working conditions to those that are available elsewhere in the economy; in fact, the reverse is more often true.

Greider is particularly wrong in thinking that global capitalism inevitably generates excess supply. This is the book's key argument and ultimately the main reason Greider believes the system will self-destruct. Consider his discussion of Boeing's outsourcing of some of its components to the Xian Aircraft Company in China (155):

> [W]hen new production work was moved to Xian from places like the United States, the global system was, in effect, swapping highly paid industrial workers for very cheap ones. To put the point more crudely, Boeing was exchanging a $50,000 American machinist for a Chinese machinist who earned $600 or $700 a year. Which one could buy the world's goods? Thus, even though incomes and purchasing power were expanding robustly among the new consumers of China,

the overall effect was an erosion of the world's potential purchasing power. If one multiplied the Xian example across many factories and industrial sectors, as well as other aspiring countries, one could begin to visualize why global consumption was unable to keep up with global production.

The argument makes little sense, as any economist could point out. The Chinese worker who earns only a tiny fraction of his American counterpart will likely demonstrate commensurately lower productivity. Even if this were not the case and the Chinese workers' wages were repressed below what their productivity ought to bring them, the result is a *transfer* in purchasing power—to Boeing's shareholders and the Chinese employers—and not a diminution of purchasing power. Perhaps Greider is thinking that Boeing's shareholders and the Chinese employers have a lower propensity to consume than the Chinese workers. But if this is Greider's reasoning, where is the argument and the evidence? Where is the global surplus in savings and the secular decline in real interest rates that we would surely have observed if income was shifting from low savers to high savers?

It may be unfair to pick on Greider, especially as some of his other conclusions are worth taking seriously. But the misunderstandings that his book displays are commonplace in the globalization debate and do not advance it. Professional economists have a duty to expose these misunderstandings and explicate them to a broader audience. But to become true honest brokers, economists must demonstrate more modesty, less condescension, and a willingness to broaden their focus.

The Role of Labor Advocates

There should be little doubt in the reader's mind by now that I am sympathetic to the difficulties experienced by workers in a globalized economy. Indeed, much of this book is devoted to arguing that, where low-skilled or less-educated workers are concerned, trade operates in a less benign fashion than most trade economists concede. Policymakers have to be cognizant of this and design their trade and other policies accordingly. But there is a major responsibility here for labor groups as well.

The political salience of labor's voice in the United States (and to a lesser extent in Europe) is currently diminished by at least three forces. First, the same pressures that reduce the bargaining power of labor in the workplace also reduce its power in the political marketplace. As governments increasingly compete for footloose enterprises and capital, the interests of workers (who after all have nowhere else to go) are relegated to second place. "Competitiveness" becomes another word for labor costs, something that can be enhanced by slashing benefits and wages. Second, the excessive attachment of labor to a single political party in the United States (and the United Kingdom) diminishes its political power. Political parties are naturally more responsive to the interests of those who are ready to shift their allegiances to competing parties than they are to the interests of captive groups.[4] Third, the receptivity of the general public to the ideas of labor advocates is greatly reduced by the protectionist tenor that too often characterizes these ideas.

Labor groups cannot do much about the first of these factors. The second may also be difficult to change. Where labor advocates can make the greatest difference is in distancing themselves from protectionist ideas. This would result in the advocacy of a more pragmatic and therefore more productive approach to trade policy. It would also lay the groundwork for the political repositioning needed to make political parties from *both* ends of the spectrum compete for the support of labor. Hence jettisoning protectionist ideas would not only serve labor interests better, it would also enhance labor's political power.

These protectionist ideas find expression most frequently in complaints about "low-wage, low-cost competition" from developing countries. But such broad condemnations of trade miss the mark. They ignore the fact that much of the difference in labor costs is typically due to lower levels of labor productivity in the exporting countries. Wages in a poor exporting country that are one-tenth the US level do not disadvantage workers in the United States when labor productivity in that country is also lower by a factor of 10.[5] More broadly, gaps in labor costs that are due to differences in the relative abundance of labor across countries are the foundation for the gains from trade. It makes as little sense to restrict trade for this reason alone as it does to restrict technological progress.

Consider, for example, the following statement by an AFL-CIO representative:

> We spend a great deal of time talking about free trade and comparative advantages, and so forth, and I am sure these are important concepts and certainly we in the US labor movement subscribe to them. Labor has benefited greatly from freeness and free trade, not only internationally, but domestically, from the comparative advantages that result from having a productive society as large and as diverse as we do in the United States, but the American labor movement has always taken the position that, *to the maximum extent possible, labor costs should be removed from that equation*, because labor is more than just a cost of production. Labor involves human dignity; it involves another whole dimension than does capital or interest or the other factors of production, and it therefore has to be treated very differently from them. (cited by Leebron 1996, note 67, emphasis added)

"Removing labor costs from the equation," as this statement calls for, would remove the primary source of comparative advantage for develop-

---

4. See Dixit and Londregan (forthcoming) for a theoretical model that explicates this outcome.

5. Freeman (1994b) finds that approximately 80 percent of the difference in hourly pay between the United States and Mexico is accounted for by differences in the skill mix of labor in the two countries and by differences in the purchasing power of wages.

ing countries *and* would deprive the US economy of the gains from trade arising from it.

To the extent that there are concerns about fairness, the issue is not labor costs per se, but how they are determined. Popular discussions of trade often gloss over this distinction. In any case, the main competitive threat to US labor, except in some highly labor-intensive sectors, comes from workers in other advanced countries, many of which have labor standards and benefit levels that are superior to those in the United States.

Hence the labor movement cannot afford to be—or to be perceived as being—against trade. This requires recognition by labor unions that imports go together with exports. One cannot be in favor of exports and against imports without committing mercantilist fallacies. Similarly, labor advocates have to accept that trade deficits are the consequence of macroeconomic realities; they have little to do with trade policies abroad, and they cannot be corrected by trade restrictions at home. The sooner the labor movement sheds such misconceptions, the sooner it will find allies in the economics and policy community.

Labor should advocate a global economy that carries a more humane face—one that recognizes national diversity and leaves room for national differences in institutions. Domestically, it should work toward labor-market institutions that enhance the mobility of workers and reduce the risks they face (some ideas toward this end are suggested below).

The Role of National Governments

Policymakers have to steer a difficult middle course between responding to the concerns discussed here and sheltering groups from foreign competition through protectionism. I can offer no hard-and-fast rules here, only some guiding principles.

Strike a Balance between Openness and Domestic Needs

This book has argued that there is often a trade-off between maintaining open borders to trade and maintaining social cohesion. When the conflict arises—when new liberalization initiatives are under discussion, for example—it makes little sense to sacrifice social concerns completely for the sake of liberalization. Put differently, as policymakers sort out economic and social objectives, free trade policies are not automatically entitled to first priority.

Thanks to many rounds of multilateral trade liberalization, tariff and nontariff restrictions on goods and many services are now at extremely low levels in the industrial countries. Most major developing countries have also slashed their trade barriers, often unilaterally and in conformity with their own domestic reforms. Most economists would agree that the efficiency benefits of further reductions in these existing barriers are unlikely to be large. Indeed, the dirty little secret of international economics is that a tiny bit of protection reduces efficiency only a tiny bit. A logical implication is that the case for further liberalization in the traditional area of manufactured goods is rather weak.[6]

Moreover, there is a case for taking greater advantage of the World Trade Organization's existing escape clause, which allows countries to institute otherwise-illegal trade restrictions under specified conditions, as well as for broadening the scope of these multilateral safeguard actions (see discussion below). In recent years, trade policy in the United States and the European Union has gone in a rather different direction, with increased use of antidumping measures and limited recourse to escape clause actions. This is likely because WTO rules and domestic legislation make the petitioning industry's job much easier in antidumping cases: there are lower evidentiary hurdles than in escape clause actions,[7] no determinate time limit, and no requirement for compensation for affected trade partners, as the escape clause provides. Also, escape clause actions, unlike antidumping duties, require presidential approval in the United States. This is an undesirable situation because antidumping rules are, on the whole, consistent neither with economics principles nor, as discussed below, with fairness. Tightening the rules on antidumping in conjunction with a reconsideration and reinvigoration of the escape clause mechanism would make a lot of sense.[8]

Do Not Neglect Social Insurance

Policymakers have to bear in mind the important role that the provision of social insurance, through social programs, has played historically in enabling multilateral liberalization and an explosion of world trade. As the welfare state is being pruned, there is a real danger that this contribution will be forgotten.

This does not mean that fiscal policy has to be profligate and budget deficits large. Nor does it mean a bigger government role. Enhanced levels of social insurance, for better labor-market outcomes, can be provided in most countries within existing levels of spending. This can be done, for

---

6. Of course, since trade barriers are still higher elsewhere than in the United States, multilateral liberalization would generate relatively greater trade opportunities for the United States. See Bergsten (1996) for an argument that emphasizes this "asymmetric" nature of the benefits.

7. In the United States, escape clause action requires demonstration of "serious injury" rather than "material injury," the latter being the lower threshold, which applies to antidumping. WTO rules also require that escape clause actions be nondiscriminatory, unlike antidumping, which can apply to any particular exporting country. Of course, an antidumping action requires a demonstration that there is dumping, but in practice US Commerce Department criteria for what constitutes "dumping" are not at all restrictive.

8. This was one of the options considered by Schott (1990).

example, by shifting the composition of income transfers from old-age insurance (i.e., social security) to labor-market insurance (i.e., unemployment compensation, trade adjustment assistance, training programs). Because pensions typically constitute the largest item of social spending in the advanced industrial countries, better targeting of this sort is highly compatible with responsible fiscal policies. Gearing social insurance more directly toward labor markets, without increasing the overall tax burden, would be one key step toward alleviating the insecurities associated with globalization.

There is a widespread feeling in many countries that, in the words of Tanzi and Schuknecht (1995, 17), "[s]ocial safety nets have ... been transformed into universal benefits with widespread free-riding behavior, and social insurance has frequently become an income support system with special interests making any effective reform very difficult." Further, "various government performance indicators suggest that the growth in spending after 1960 may not have brought about significantly improved economic performance or greater social progress" (1995, 20). However, this book has suggested that social spending has had the important function of buying social peace. Without disagreeing about the need to eliminate waste and reform in the welfare state more broadly, I would argue that the need for social insurance does not decline but rather increases as global integration increases. So the message to reformers of the social welfare system is, don't throw the baby out with the bath water.[9]

Do Not Use "Competitiveness" as an Excuse for Domestic Reform

One of the reasons globalization gets a bad rap is that policymakers often fall into the trap of using "competitiveness" as an excuse for needed domestic reforms. Large fiscal deficits or lagging domestic productivity are problems that drag living standards down in many industrial countries and would do so even in closed economies. Indeed, the term "competitiveness" itself is largely meaningless when applied to whole economies, unless it is used to refer to things that already have a proper name—such as productivity, investment, and economic growth. Too often, however, the need to resolve fiscal or productivity problems is presented to the electorate as the consequence of global competitive pressures. This not only makes the required policies a harder sell—why should we adjust just for the sake of becoming better competitors against the Koreans or the Mexicans?—it also erodes the domestic support for international

---

9. Many economists would agree that the amount of resources needed to keep the most disadvantaged from falling through the cracks is actually not that big. Krugman (1996) cites a figure of 2 percent of GDP. In absolute terms, this is, of course, a lot of money, but it is less than half of what an average OECD country spends on servicing the public debt each year.

trade—if we have to do all these painful things because of trade, maybe trade isn't such a wonderful thing anyhow!

The French strikes of 1995 are a good case in point. What made the opposition to the proposed fiscal and pension reforms particularly salient was the perception that fundamental changes in the French way of life were being imposed for the sake of international economic integration. The French government presented the reforms as required by the Maastricht criteria, which they were. But presumably, the Maastricht criteria themselves reflected the policymakers' belief that a smaller welfare state would serve their economies better in the longer run. By and large, the French government did not make the case for reform on its own strengths. By using the Maastricht card, it turned the discussion into a debate on European economic integration. Hence the widespread public reaction, which extended beyond just those workers whose fates would be immediately affected.

The lesson for policymakers is, do not sell reforms that are good for the economy and the citizenry as reforms that are dictated by international economic integration.

Do Not Abuse "Fairness" Claims in Trade

The notion of fairness in trade is not as vacuous as many economists think. Consequently, nations have the right—and should be allowed—to restrict trade when it conflicts with *widely held* norms at home or undermines domestic social arrangements that enjoy *broad* support.

But there is much that is done in the name of "fair trade" that falls far short of this criterion. There are two sets of practices in particular that should be immediately suspect. One concerns complaints made against other nations when very similar practices abound at home. Antidumping proceedings are a clear example: standard business practices, such as pricing over the life of a product or pricing over the business cycle, can result in duties being imposed on an exporting firm. There is nothing "unfair" about these business practices, as is made abundantly clear by the fact that domestic firms engage in them as well.

The second category concerns cases in which other nations are unilaterally asked to change *their* domestic practices so as to equalize competitive conditions. Japan is frequently at the receiving end of such demands from the United States and the European Union. A more recent example concerns the declaration by the US Trade Representative that corruption in foreign countries will henceforth be considered as unfair trade. While considerations of fairness and legitimacy will guide a country's own social arrangements, even by restricting imports if need be, such considerations should not allow one country to impose its own institutions on others. Proponents of fair trade must bear this key distinction in mind. Thus, it is perfectly legitimate for the United States to make it illegal for domestic firms to engage in corrupt practices abroad (as was done with the Foreign Corrupt Practices Act of 1977). It is also legitimate to negotiate a multilateral set of principles with other countries in the Organization for Economic Cooperation and Development (OECD) with broadly similar norms. It may also be legitimate to restrict imports from a country whose labor practices broad segments of the domestic population deem offensive. But it is not acceptable to unilaterally threaten retaliation against other countries because their business practices do not comply with domestic standards at home *in order to force these countries to alter their own standards.*[10] Using claims of fairness to advance competitive aims is coercive and inherently contradictory. Trying to "export" norms by asking other countries to alter their social arrangements to match domestic ones is inappropriate for the same reason.

The Role of International Institutions

One area in which international cooperation can be helpful has already been mentioned: the ability of firms to play national tax authorities off each other is a source of negative cross-border externality, as it undercuts the revenue sources needed to maintain social and political cohesion and ultimately erodes support for free trade. Greater exchange of information among tax authorities would be one small step in the right direction. Negotiating an international convention to restrict international firms' ability to evade taxation via foreign investment would constitute a more ambitious effort, but one that would have a greater chance of making a difference.

There is a growing realization among governments that something along these lines may need to be done. Concern about the revenue consequences of tax competition recently led the OECD to set up a task force (with priority funding) on curbing such competition among its member states. As the OECD statement recognizes, globalization "opens up the risk of competitive bidding between countries for mobile business." The task force's first task is to "examine criteria for distinguishing between fair and harmful tax competition."[11] To be fully effective, such an effort

---

10. It may be that restricting imports will cause the exporting country to alter its practices, irrespective of whether that was the stated goal of the policy. But that does not make the distinction any less valid. The motives that drive trade policy in the advanced industrial countries are usually transparent. There is little doubt that the Foreign Corrupt Practices Act of 1977, for example, was motivated by domestic ethical considerations, while many US and European complaints against Japan and some developing countries are clearly driven by a desire to make "them" more like "us." How foreign trade partners choose to react to policies of the first kind (the "legitimate" actions, that is) is their own business.

11. The quotes are from the OECD's Internet statement on the project (see www.oecd.org/daf/fa/taxcomp.htm; *Financial Times*, 13 January 1997, 16).

has to enlist the cooperation of non-OECD countries as well. This is implicit in the OECD's approach, as its task force is slated to look at practices in such tax havens as the Cayman Islands as well as the more modest preferential tax regimes of countries such as Ireland, the Netherlands, and Belgium (*Financial Times*, 13 January 1997, 16).

More broadly, the arguments made in this book have two somewhat conflicting implications for multilateral institutions. On the one hand, these institutions must encourage greater convergence of policies and standards ("deep integration") *among willing countries* to help reduce tensions arising from differences in national practices.[12] On the other, they must make room for selective disengagement from multilateral disciplines, under well-specified contingencies, for countries that need breathing room to satisfy domestic requirements that are in conflict with liberalizing trade.

The apparent tension between these two objectives is partly reconciled by the caveat in the previous sentence. These organizations will need to set up a well-defined and multilaterally agreed set of hurdles that must be cleared before a nation can exercise the selective disengagement in question—be it higher tariffs, a quota, or an exemption from harmonization requirements. In other words, there need to be multilateral rules on how one can depart from multilateral rules![13]

Of course, this is what the escape clause mechanism under the WTO, and before it the General Agreement on Tariffs and Trade (GATT), is in principle all about. But the mechanism has not served its purpose well. Governments have preferred other measures to the GATT's safeguard mechanism. Hence "gray area" measures, such as voluntary export restraints (VERs), proliferated before the Uruguay Round ended, and there has been an explosion of antidumping cases. There were only 150 official safeguard actions under the GATT (through 1994) but more than 1,000 antidumping cases at the national level between 1985 and 1992 alone (Hoekman and Kostecki 1995, chapter 7). Antidumping procedures are

---

12. Lawrence, Bressand, and Ito (1996) argue for the creation of a series of "clubs" among partners willing to engage in deeper integration in areas not well covered in the WTO—such as competition policy or environment. This would be a departure from unconditional multilateralism and would risk institutionalizing discriminatory treatment of trade partners. I would prefer to see the WTO used for these new areas, with a more effective escape clause as a safety valve (see discussion below).

13. It is recognized in the theory of repeated games that sustaining cooperation among players throughout a long (infinite) horizon when there are shocks to the system may require periods of "noncooperation." An appropriate multilateral trading regime will recognize this and incorporate "safety valves" into its rules—that is, exemptions from its requirements under specified contingencies. See Bagwell and Staiger (1990) for a formal model that justifies the escape clause in these terms. In the context of such models, my argument is that social conflicts result in a greater temptation to "defect" during bad times and hence require a more accessible escape clause to render long-term cooperation sustainable.

today effectively serving as the safeguard mechanism of choice. This subverts the trade regime, gives safeguards a bad name, and crowds out an effective outlet for legitimate concerns.

Hence, a revamped and expanded safeguards clause, along with tighter restrictions on the use of antidumping, would be well worth considering.[14] By broadening the current Agreement on Safeguards, WTO members can then allay US and EU fears of import surges, which have so far prevented the reining in of antidumping measures.

Currently, the Agreement on Safeguards allows temporary increases in trade restrictions under a very narrow set of conditions. It requires a determination that *increased* imports "cause or threaten to cause serious injury to the domestic industry"[15] and that causality is firmly established. Furthermore, injury cannot be attributed solely to imports if there are multiple causes for it.[16] Safeguards cannot be applied to developing-country exporters unless their share of imports of the product concerned is above a given threshold. A country applying safeguard measures has to compensate the affected exporters by providing "equivalent concessions," lacking which the exporter is free to retaliate.

A broader interpretation of safeguards would acknowledge that countries may legitimately wish to restrict trade for reasons going beyond competitive threats to their industries. Distributional concerns or conflicts with domestic norms or social arrangements are among such legitimate reasons. One could imagine recasting the current agreement into an Agreement on *Social* Safeguards, which would permit the application of safeguard measures under a broader range of circumstances. This would require recasting the "serious injury" test. I would replace the injury criterion with another hurdle: the need to demonstrate broad domestic support, *among all concerned parties*, for the proposed safeguard measure.

To see how that might work in practice, consider what the current agreement says:

> A Member may apply a safeguard measure only following an investigation by the competent authorities of that Member pursuant to procedures previously established and made public in consonance with Article X of the GATT 1994. This investigation shall include reasonable public notice to all interested parties and public hearings or other appropriate means in which *importers, exporters and other*

---

14. A refurbished escape clause, under which all trade relief would be centered, was proposed in Hufbauer and Rosen (1986). See also Perez-Lopez for a similar approach (1989). My discussion of the expanded safeguards clause is based on earlier work reported in Rodrik (1995).

15. Serious injury is defined as "a significant overall impairment in the position of a domestic industry."

16. According to the agreement, "When factors other than increased imports are causing injury to the domestic industry at the same time, such injury shall not be attributed to increased imports."

interested parties could present evidence and their views, including the opportunity
to respond to the presentations of other parties and to submit their views, inter
alia, as to *whether or not the application of a safeguard measure would be in the public
interest* [emphasis added]. The competent authorities shall publish a report setting
forth their findings and reasoned conclusions reached on all pertinent issues of
fact and law.

The main shortcoming of this clause is that while it allows all relevant
groups, exporters and importers in particular, to air their views, it does
not actually compel them to do so. Consequently, it results in a strong
bias in the domestic investigative process toward the interests of import-
competing groups, which are the petitioners for import relief and its
obvious beneficiaries. Indeed, this is a key problem with hearings in
antidumping proceedings, where testimony from other groups besides
the import-competing industry is not allowed.

A key reform, then, would be to require those conducting the investiga-
tions in each country to gather testimony and views from *all* relevant
parties, including consumer and public interest groups, importers of the
products concerned, and exporters to the affected country, and to determine whether there exists *broad support* among these groups for the application of the safeguard measure in question. The requirement that groups
whose incomes would be hurt by imposing trade restrictions—importers
and exporters—be compelled to testify and that the investigative body
determine whether these groups also support the safeguard measure
would ensure that protectionism pure and simple would not have much
chance of success. At the same time, when deeply and widely held social
norms are at stake, these groups are unlikely to oppose safeguards in a
public manner, as this would endanger their standing among the public
at large. Imagine, for example, that slave labor is used in producing goods
for export in a given country. It is difficult to believe that exporters to
that country would publicly defend trade with it.

The main advantage of the proposed procedure is that it would force
a public debate on the legitimacy of trade and on the appropriateness of
restricting it. It ensures that all sides would be heard. This rarely happens
in practice, unless the trade partner in question is an important one.[17]
This procedure could also be complemented with a strengthened monitoring and surveillance role for the WTO to ensure that domestic procedures
are in compliance with the expanded safeguard clause. An automatic sunset
clause could ensure that trade restrictions do not become entrenched long
after their perceived need has disappeared.

Broadening safeguard actions in this manner would not be without its
risks. One has to take into account the possibility that the new procedures

---

17. The public debate that surrounds the US president's annual decision on whether to
extend China's most-favored nation trade status is a good example. In my view, this debate
serves a useful function.

would be abused for protectionist ends and that the door to unilateral action on a broad front would be opened, despite the high threshold envisaged here. But inaction is not without risk either. Absent creative thinking and novel institutional designs, the tensions created by globalization may spark a new set of "gray area" measures entirely outside multilateral disciplines. That would be far worse than the revised safeguard regime described here.

Concluding Remarks

Globalization is not occurring in a vacuum. It is part of a broader trend that we may call marketization. Receding government, deregulation, and the shrinking of social obligations are the domestic counterparts of the intertwining of national economies. Globalization could not have advanced this far without these complementary forces. The broader challenge for the 21st century is to engineer a new balance between market and society, one that will continue to unleash the creative energies of private entrepreneurship without eroding the social basis of cooperation.

The tensions between globalization and social cohesion are real, and they are unlikely to disappear of their own accord. The proposals in this chapter are little more than a beginning, and perhaps not even that. There is no magic formula that can be applied. Indeed, part of the difficulty in thinking prescriptively about these issues is that some of the basic analytical and empirical work on the consequences of globalization remains to be done. Contrary to what many economists believe, we lack a full understanding of how globalization works.

"What is actually required to make progress with novel problems a society encounters," writes Albert Hirschman, "is political entrepreneurship, imagination, patience here, impatience there, and other varieties of virtù and fortuna. . ." (1994, 25). We need all of these, plus a good dose of pragmatism, to make progress on the challenges ahead.

Appendices

Appendix A

I will use a very simple model to sharpen the logic of the argument in chapter 4. I assume a small, open economy that produces (and exports) a single good, whose price is determined in world markets. This good is produced under constant returns to scale and using labor and capital. Unlike labor, capital can move across borders, but at a cost. The magnitude of this cost will be captured in a parameter for the degree of "openness" of the economy. Labor, whose welfare will be the focus of the analysis, consumes only the importable. The only source of uncertainty in the model is the terms of trade (the price of exports relative to the price of imports), which is assumed to be stochastic. Labor income consists of wage income plus the proceeds of a tax on domestic capital. To make the point as sharply as possible, I assume that the government maximizes domestic capitalists' welfare subject to a reservation level of utility for workers and chooses the tax on capital accordingly.

I will use the model to show the following. An increase in openness makes domestic capital more responsive to changes in international prices and correspondingly magnifies the amplitude of fluctuations in real wages at home. Hence labor becomes worse off, due to increased exposure to risk, even if the mean (expected) real wage remains unchanged. To restore the expected utility of workers to its reservation level, the government has to increase income transfers and raise the tax on capital. This strategy works as long as the openness of the economy and the international mobility of capital are not too high. However, when openness crosses a certain threshold, an attempt to compensate labor by increasing the tax on capital becomes self-defeating. Past that threshold, the flight of capital and the erosion of real wages at home would more than offset the value of income transfers. In an extremely open economy, therefore, the government loses its ability to compensate workers through the tax system, and the constraint that workers' utility be above a certain reservation level can no longer be satisfied. One "solution" would be to make it more costly for capital to move abroad.

Let the production function of the export sector be written as $f(k, l)$, with the usual regularity conditions: $f_k > 0$, $f_l > 0$, $f_{kk} < 0$, $f_{ll} < 0$, and $f_{kl} > 0$. We normalize the economy's fixed labor endowment to unity, so the production function can also be expressed as $f(k)$. The domestically owned capital stock is exogenously fixed at k_0. Note that k, the capital used at home, can differ from k_0 as capital moves in and out of the country. A key assumption is that an increasing cost is incurred by capitalists as capital moves across borders. We can think of this as the cost of setting up business in a less familiar environment, of transporting the final goods back to the home economy, and of communicating with subsidiaries in a different country, among other things. Increased globalization will be captured in the model by reductions in λ.

Let p stand for the relative price of the exported good or service. The model is described in three equations:

$$r = pf_k(k) - \tau \tag{A.1}$$

$$r = r^* - \lambda(k_0 - k) \tag{A.2}$$

$$w = pf_l(k) \tag{A.3}$$

The domestic return to capital (r) is given by the marginal value product of capital, net of the domestic tax. International trade in capital services requires that this return be equal to the international return (r^*) minus a margin that is related to the cost of moving capital abroad. Hence a capital outflow that reduces the capital stock at home to k_1 would depress the rate of return earned by domestic capitalists to $r^* - \lambda(k_0 - k_1)$. The second equation expresses this arbitrage condition. Finally, the third equation states that the domestic wage (w) equals the marginal value product of labor. These three equations determine the three endogenous variables in the system, w, r, and k.

Figure A.1 depicts how the model works. The downward sloping schedule shows the negative relationship between r and k expressed in equation (A.1). As the relative price of the export (p) moves around, so does this schedule. Intuitively, the return to capital fluctuates in tandem with the world price of the export. The upward-sloping schedule in turn represents the relationship expressed in equation (A.2). Two versions of this schedule are shown, one for high λ (low globalization) and one for low λ (high globalization). The lower is λ, the flatter this schedule. In the limit, with

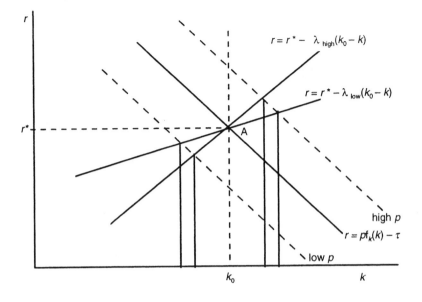

capital fully mobile at zero cost, the schedule would be horizontal, and it would fix the domestic rate of return at r^*.

Denote by $k(p, \tau, \lambda)$ the equilibrium level of capital employed at home. Consider an initial equilibrium in which the combination of parameters is such that $k(p, \tau, \lambda) = k_0$. In this equilibrium, denoted by point A in figure A.1, $r = r^*$. Changes in λ would have no effect on w or k (or r) starting from this initial equilibrium, since

$$\frac{dk}{d\lambda} = \frac{k - k_0}{pf_{kk} - \lambda},$$

$$\frac{dw}{d\lambda} = pf_{kl}\left[\frac{k - k_0}{pf_{kk} - \lambda}\right]$$

and both expressions equal zero when $k = k_0$. Intuitively, we fix the initial equilibrium such that capital has no incentive to move in or out of the domestic economy, and consequently changes in the cost of mobility are of no consequence.

Now consider what happens as p fluctuates. A reduction in p drives down the domestic return to capital and results in a capital outflow, the magnitude of which is inversely proportional to λ. As the figure demonstrates, the greater the mobility of capital, the wider the fluctuations in the domestic capital stock in response to changes in the world price. Formally,

$$\frac{dk}{dp} = \frac{f_k}{\lambda - pf_{kk}} > 0,$$

which is decreasing in λ. The consequences for labor can be easily deduced. Because the domestic wage (in terms of the imported good) is determined by the value marginal product of labor in the exported good (equation A.3), capital mobility accentuates the fluctuation in the consumption wage. The lower is λ, the wider the amplitude of fluctuations in w:

$$\frac{dw}{dp} = f_l + \frac{pf_{kl}f_k}{\lambda - pf_{kk}} > 0,$$

which is decreasing in λ.

In fact, things are even worse for labor insofar as part of workers' income comes from the tax on capital. Denoting workers' total (real) income by I,

$$I = w + \tau k \qquad (A.4)$$

Fluctuations in I therefore result not only from fluctuations in wages, but also from fluctuations in the tax base (k) as capital moves back and forth in search of higher returns.

Now consider the effect of changing the tax on capital, holding world prices constant. We have

$$\frac{dI}{d\tau} = k + \left[\frac{dw}{d\tau} + \tau\frac{dk}{d\tau} \right]$$

$$= k - \frac{\tau + pf_{kl}}{\lambda - pf_{kl}}$$

This expression is increasing in λ, indicating that the tax on capital is most effective as a redistributive tool when capital cannot move abroad easily. For values of λ sufficiently close to zero, on the other hand, $dI/d\tau$ can be shown to be unambiguously negative for any strictly positive level of τ.[1] The implication is that an increase in the tax on capital will enhance workers' incomes in a situation in which globalization is low but reduce it when globalization is high. This plays a key role in the argument.

Consider the following timing of events:

- λ is determined;

- the government sets τ to maximize capitalists' income subject to a reservation level of (expected) utility for workers;

---

1. This follows from setting $\lambda = 0$ and noting that $kf_{kk} + f_{kl} = 0$.

- p is revealed;

- the equilibrium levels of w, r, and k are determined.

Since τ is selected before p is revealed, the government must take into account the stochastic properties of p and how uncertainty affects workers' expected utility.

Assume that p is a random variable with a mean $\bar{p}$ and a standard deviation σ. Let $I(p, \tau, \lambda)$ stand for the realized equilibrium value of income. Taking a Taylor expansion around $\bar{p}$, expected utility, $EV(I[p, \tau, \lambda])$, can be approximated in the following manner:

$$EV[I(p, \tau, \lambda)] = E\left[V(I([\bar{p}, \tau, \lambda]) + \frac{dV(I[\bar{p}, \tau, \lambda])}{dp}(p - \bar{p}) \right.$$

$$\left. + \frac{1}{2}\frac{d^2V(I[\bar{p}, \tau, \lambda])}{dp^2}(p - \bar{p})^2 \right]$$

$$= V(I(\bar{p}, \tau, \lambda) + \frac{1}{2}\frac{d^2V[I(\bar{p}, \tau, \lambda)]}{dp^2}\sigma^2$$

Now assume that workers' utility (V) is logarithmic:

$$V(I) = \log I = \log (w + \tau k)$$

Expected utility can then be written as:

$$EV[I(p, \tau, \lambda)] = \log [w(\bar{p}, \tau, \lambda) + \tau k(\bar{p}, \tau, \lambda)]$$

$$- \frac{1}{2} [w(\bar{p}, \tau, \lambda) + \tau k(\bar{p}, \tau, \lambda)]^{-2}$$

$$\left[f_l(k[\bar{p}, \tau, \lambda]) + f_k(k[\bar{p}, \tau, \lambda])\frac{\tau + pf_{kl}(k[\bar{p}, \tau, \lambda])}{\lambda - pf_{kk}(k[\bar{p}, \tau, \lambda])} \right]^2 \sigma^2$$

Since the utility function is concave in income, and hence workers are risk-averse, expected utility is decreasing in the variance of the world price. Moreover, an increase in openness increases the weight received by price volatility and reduces expected utility *ceteris paribus*. This can be seen by evaluating this expression at an equilibrium at which $k = k_0$ (so that w and k are insensitive to changes in λ) and by noting that a reduction in λ increases the second (negative) term in absolute value. The reason for this has been discussed above: enhanced mobility of capital magnifies the fluctuations in workers' income for any given change in p.

Note that this effect is purely a consequence of increased exposure to risk and is independent of any other consequences of openness. If

Figure A.2

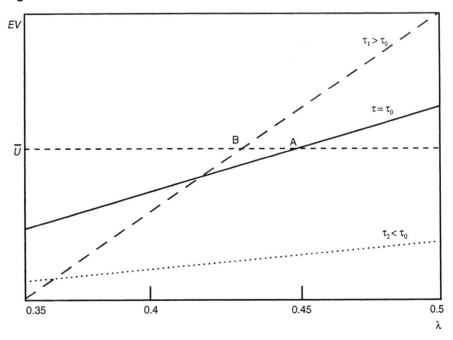

increased openness further translated into a capital outflow, the losses to workers would, of course, be greater. Conversely, if increased openness were to reduce the relative price of imports (a channel from which we have abstracted), there would be a compensating gain.

As mentioned above, the government is assumed to operate under a constraint that puts a floor below the expected utility of workers:

$$EV[(I(p, \tau, \lambda)] \geq U$$

Let the initial levels of τ and λ be τ_0 and λ_0. As before, assume that the domestic capital stock is such that $k(\bar{p}, \tau_0, \lambda_0) = k_0$. It is convenient to assume further that the above constraint just binds in this equilibrium. This is shown as point A in figure A.2. The figure shows the consequences of a reduction in λ. As discussed above, expected utility falls as λ decreases. For some range of λ, the government can compensate for the reduction in workers' expected utility by raising τ. At point B, for example, workers have the same level of expected utility as at A, thanks to an increase in the tax from τ_0 to τ_1. However, as the figure shows, once the cost of moving capital abroad becomes sufficiently small, this is no longer a viable strategy. Neither an increase nor a decrease in τ can fully compensate for the loss in expected utility suffered as a result of a fall in λ. Consequently, for sufficiently high degrees of "globalization," the government can no longer meet the constraint on workers' utility.

What might then happen is left outside the model. But it is reasonable to think that the government would come under severe pressure from workers to restrict international economic integration (for instance, by imposing taxes on firms that move abroad).

Appendix B

Table B.1 List of variables and sources[a]

Variable	Definition	Source
AREA	Land area	Barro and Lee 1994
ASIAE	Dummy for East Asian countries	Barro and Lee 1994
CGAVGxxyy	Real government consumption as a percentage of GDP	PWT 5.6a
DEPEND90	Dependency ratio	WD
GDPSH5xx	Real per capita GDP	Barro and Lee 1994
LAAM	Dummy for Latin American countries	Barro and Lee 1994
OECD	Dummy for OECD countries	Barro and Lee 1994
OPENAVGxxyy	Exports plus imports divided by GDP	PWT 5.6a
SAFRICA	Dummy for sub-Saharan African countries	Barro and Lee 1994
SOC	Dummy for socialist countries	Sachs and Warner 1995
TOTDLOGSTD	Standard deviation of log differences in terms of trade, 71-90	WD
URBAN90	Urbanization rate	WD

a. "xx" refers to year 19xx, while "xxyy" refers to an average during 19xx-19yy (unless specified otherwise). All government expenditure and revenue data are expressed as a percentage of GDP or GNP. "PWT 5.6" stands for Penn World Tables Mark 5.6a; "WD" for *World Data 1995* (World Bank).

References

Alesina, Alberto, and Roberto Perotti. 1995. "The Welfare State and Competitiveness." Unpublished paper.

Alesina, Alberto, and Dani Rodrik. 1994. "Distributive Politics and Economic Growth." *Quarterly Journal of Economics* 109, no. 2 (May): 465-90.

Bagwell, Kyle, and Robert W. Staiger. 1990. "A Theory of Managed Trade." *American Economic Review* 4: 779-95.

Bairoch, Paul, and Richard Kozul-Wright. 1996. "Globalization Myths: Some Historical Reflections on Integration, Industrialization, and Growth in the World Economy." Discussion Paper No. 113. United Nations Conference on Trade and Development.

Barro, Robert J., and Jong-Wha Lee. 1994. "Data Set for a Panel of 138 Countries." Harvard University, Cambridge, MA, January. Unpublished manuscript.

Bergsten, C. Fred. 1996. "Globalizing Free Trade." *Foreign Affairs* 75, no. 3 (May / June): 105-20.

Bergsten, C. Fred, and Marcus Noland. 1993. *Reconcilable Differences? United States-Japan Economic Conflict.* Washington: Institute for International Economics.

Berman, Eli, Stephen Machin, and John Bound. 1996. "Implications of Skill-Biased Technological Change: International Evidence." Boston University. Photocopy.

Bhagwati, Jagdish N. 1988. *Protectionism.* Cambridge, MA: MIT Press.

Bhagwati, Jagdish N. 1991. *Free Traders and Free Immigrationists: Strangers or Friends?* Working Paper No. 20. New York: Russell Sage Foundation.

Bhagwati, Jagdish N. 1996. "A New Epoch?" Columbia University. Unpublished book review.

Bhagwati, Jagdish N., and Vivek H. Dehejia. 1994. "Freer Trade and Wages of the Unskilled— Is Marx Striking Again?" In Jagdish N. Bhagwati and Marvin H. Kosters, *Trade and Wages: Leveling Wages Down?* Washington: American Enterprise Institute.

Bhagwati, Jagdish N., and Robert E. Hudec, eds. 1996. *Fair Trade and Harmonization: Prerequisites for Free Trade?, vol. 1: Economic Analysis.* Cambridge, MA: MIT Press.

Blanchflower, David G., Andrew J. Oswald, and Peter Sanfey. 1996. "Wages, Profits, and Rent-Sharing." *Quarterly Journal of Economics* 111, no. 1 (February): 227-52.

Borjas, George, Richard Freeman, and Lawrence Katz. 1992. "On the Labor Market Effects of Immigration and Trade." In Borjas and Freeman, *Immigration and the Work Force.* Chicago: University of Chicago Press.

Borjas, George, and Valerie Ramey. 1994. "The Relationship between Wage Inequality and International Trade." In Jeffrey Bergstrand et al., *The Changing Distribution of Income in an Open U.S. Economy.* Amsterdam: North-Holland.

Borjas, George, and Valerie Ramey. 1995. "Foreign Competition, Market Power, and Wage Inequality." *Quarterly Journal of Economics* 110, no. 4 (November): 1075-110.

Bovard, James. 1991. *The Myth of Fair Trade.* Policy Analysis No. 164. Washington: Cato Institute. www.cato.org/pubs/pas/pa-164.html.

Cameron, David. 1978. "The Expansion of the Public Economy." *American Political Science Review* 72: 1243-61.

Castañeda, Jorge. 1996. "Mexico's Circle of Misery." *Foreign Affairs* 75, no. 4 (July/August): 92-105.

Cline, William R. 1997. *Trade and Wage Inequality.* Washington: Institute for International Economics. Forthcoming.

Collins, Susan, ed. 1996. *Imports, Exports, and the American Worker.* Washington: Brookings Institution.

Commission of the European Communities. 1993. *Green Paper on European Social Policy.* Com(93). November. Brussels.

Council of Economic Advisers (CEA). 1996. *Job Creation and Employment Opportunities: The United States Labor Market, 1993-1996.* Washington.

Crick, Bernard R. 1962. *In Defence of Politics.* Chicago: University of Chicago Press.

Davis, Donald R. 1996. *Does European Unemployment Prop Up American Wages?* NBER Working Paper 5620. Cambridge, MA: National Bureau of Economic Research.

Dixit, Avinash, and John Londregan. N.d. "The Determinants of Success of Special Interests in Redistributive Politics." *Journal of Politics.* Forthcoming.

Easterly, William, and Ross Levine. 1996. "Africa's Growth Tragedy: Policies and Ethnic Divisions." Washington: World Bank. Unpublished paper.

Esping-Andersen, Gösta. 1994. "Welfare State and the Economy." In Neil J. Smelser and Richard Swedberg, *The Handbook of Economic Sociology.* Princeton, NJ: Princeton University Press.

Etzioni, Amitai. 1994. *The Spirit of Community: The Reinvention of American Society.* New York: Simon & Schuster.

Farber, Henry S. 1996. *The Changing Face of Job Loss in the United States, 1981-1993.* NBER Working Paper No. 5596. Washington: National Bureau of Economic Research.

Freeman, Richard. 1994a. "A Hard-Headed Look at Labour Standards." In W. Sengenberger and D. Campbell, *International Labour Standards and Economic Interdependence.* Geneva: International Institute for Labour Studies.

Freeman, Richard. 1994b. "A Global Labor Market? Differences in Wages among Countries in the 1980s." Unpublished paper.

Freeman, Richard. 1996a. "Will Globalization Dominate U.S. Labor Market Outcomes?" In Susan Collins, *Imports, Exports, and the American Worker.* Washington: Brookings Institution.

Freeman, Richard. 1996b. "When Earnings Diverge: Causes, Consequences, and Cures for the New Inequality in the U.S." Unpublished paper.

Friedman, Thomas L. 1996. "Don't Leave Globalization's Losers Out of Mind." *International Herald Tribune* (18 July).

Garrett, Geoffrey, and Deborah Mitchell. 1996. "Globalization and the Welfare State: Income Transfers in the Industrial Democracies, 1966-1990." The Wharton School, University of Pennsylvania. Unpublished paper.

Gottschalk, Peter, and Robert Moffitt. 1994. "The Growth of Earnings Instability in the U.S. Labor Market." *Brookings Papers on Economic Activity* 2: 217-54. Washington: Brookings Institution.

Greider, Willian. 1997. *One World, Ready or Not — The Manic Logic of Global Capitalism.* New York: Simon & Schuster.

Hines, James. 1995. "Forbidden Payment: Foreign Bribery and American Business after 1977." Harvard University. Photocopy.

Hirschman, Albert O. 1994. "Social Conflict as Pillar of Democratic Society." *Political Theory* 22, no. 2 (May): 203-18.

Hoekman, Bernard M., and Michael M. Kostecki. 1995. "The Political Economy of the World Trading System." Unpublished book manuscript.

Howell, David. 1994. "The Skills Myth." *The American Prospect*, no. 18 (Summer): 81-90.

Hufbauer, Gary C., and Howard F. Rosen. 1986. *Trade Policy for Troubled Industries*. POLICY ANALYSES IN INTERNATIONAL ECONOMICS 15. Washington: Institute for International Economics.

Irwin, Douglas A. 1996. "The United States in a New Global Economy? A Century's Perspective." *American Economic Review, Papers and Proceedings* 86, no. 2 (May): 41-46.

Jaffee, Adam B., Steven R. Peterson, Paul R. Portney, and Robert Stavins. 1995. "Environmental Regulation and the Competitiveness of U.S. Manufacturing." *Journal of Economic Literature* 33, no. 1 (March): 164-78.

Kapstein, Ethan. 1996. "Workers and the World Economy." *Foreign Affairs* 75, no. 3 (May/June): 16-37.

Katz, Lawrence F., and Lawrence H. Summers. 1989. "Industry Rents: Evidence and Implications." *Brookings Papers on Economic Activity (Microeconomics)*: 209-75.

Katzenstein, Peter J. 1984. *Corporatism and Change: Austria, Switzerland, and the Politics of Industry*. Ithaca, NY, and London: Cornell University Press.

Katzenstein, Peter J. 1985. *Small States in World Markets: Industrial Policy in Europe*. Ithaca, NY, and London: Cornell University Press.

Keynes, John Maynard. 1972 [1926]. "The End of Laissez-Faire." In *The Collected Writings of John Maynard Keynes*, vol. 9. 3d ed. London: Macmillan.

Keynes, John Maynard. 1982 [1933]. "National Self-Sufficiency." In *The Collected Writings of John Maynard Keynes*, vol. 21.

Knack, Stephen, and Philip Keefer. 1996. "Does Social Capital Have an Economic Payoff? A Cross-Country Investigation." American University. Unpublished paper.

Krueger, Alan. 1996. "Observations on International Labor Standards and Trade." Princeton University. Unpublished paper.

Krugman, Paul. 1995. *Technology, Trade, and Factor Prices*. NBER Working Paper No. 5355. Cambridge, MA: National Bureau of Economic Research.

Krugman, Paul. 1996. *Pop Internationalism*. Cambridge, MA: MIT Press.

Lawrence, Robert Z. 1991. "Efficient or Exclusionist? The Import Behavior of Japanese Corporate Groups." *Brookings Papers on Economic Activity* 1: 311-31. Washington: Brookings Institution.

Lawrence, Robert Z. 1993. "Japan's Different Trade Regime: An Analysis with Particular Reference to *Keiretsu*." *Journal of Economic Perspectives* 7, no. 3 (Summer): 3-19.

Lawrence, Robert Z. 1996. *Single World, Divided Nations? International Trade and OECD Labor Markets*. Paris: Organization for Economic Cooperation and Development.

Lawrence, Robert Z., Albert Bressand, and Takatoshi Ito. 1996. *A Vision for the World Economy: Openness, Diversity, and Cohesion*. Washington: Brookings Institution.

Lawrence, Robert Z., and Matthew Slaughter. 1993. "Trade and U.S. Wages in the 1980s: Giant Sucking Sound or Small Hiccup?" *Brookings Papers on Economic Activity (Microeconomics)*: 161-210.

Leamer, Edward. 1996. "In Search of Stolper-Samuelson Effects on U.S. Wages." In Susan Collins, *Imports, Exports, and the American Worker*. Washington: Brookings Institution.

Leebron, David W. 1996. "Lying Down with Procrustes: An Analysis of Harmonization Claims." In Jagdish N. Bhagwati and Robert E. Hudec, *Fair Trade and Harmonization: Prerequisites for Free Trade?, vol. 1: Economic Analysis*. Cambridge, MA: MIT Press.

Leibfried, Stephan, and Paul Pierson. 1995. "Semisovereign Welfare States: Social Policy in a Multitiered Europe." In Stephan Leibfried and Paul Pierson, *European Social Policy: Between Fragmentation and Integration*. Washington: Brookings Institution.

Levy, Frank. 1996. "Where Did All the Money Go? A Layman's Guide to Recent Trends in U.S. Living Standards." Massachusetts Institute of Technology. Unpublished manuscript.

Lindert, Peter H. 1994. "The Rise of Social Spending." *Explorations in Economic History* 31: 1-37.

Mayer, William G. 1992. "The Shifting Sands of Public Opinion: Is Liberalism Back?" *The Public Interest*, no. 107 (Spring): 3-17.

Mendoza, Enrique G., Gian Maria Milesi-Ferretti, and Patrick Asea. 1996. *On the Effectiveness of Tax Policy in Altering Long-Run Growth: Harberger's Superneutrality Conjecture.* CEPR Discussion Paper No. 1378. London: Centre for Economic Policy Research.

Mendoza, Enrique G., Assaf Razin, and Linda L. Tesar. 1994. "Effective Tax Rates in Macroeconomics: Cross-Country Estimates of Tax Rates on Factor Incomes and Consumption." *Journal of Monetary Economics* 34 no. 3 (December): 297-323.

Mishel, Lawrence. 1995. "Rising Tides, Sinking Wages." *The American Prospect*, no. 23 (Fall): 60-64.

Mitchell, Daniel J. B. 1985. "Shifting Norms in Wage Determination." *Brookings Papers on Economic Activity* 2: 575-99. Washington: Brookings Institution.

Noland, Marcus. N.d. "Public Policy, Private Preferences, and the Japanese Trade Pattern." *Review of Economics and Statistics.* Forthcoming.

Nozick, Robert. 1974. *Anarchy, State, and Utopia.* New York: Basic Books.

Nye, Joseph. 1996. "Visions of Governance in the Twenty-First Century." Keynote speech for the Kennedy School of Government Spring Symposium, May, Harvard University.

Penn World Tables. 1995. Mark 5.6a. Online data base. Available from National Bureau of Economic Research, Cambridge, MA, and via Internet @ nber.harvard.edu.

Perez-Lopez, Jorge F. 1989. "Case for a GATT Code on Temporary Measures." *The World Economy* 12, no. 1 (March): 53-67.

Perotti, Roberto. 1996. "Inefficient Redistribution." Columbia University. Unpublished paper.

Polanyi, Karl. 1944. *The Great Transformation.* Boston, MA: Beacon Press.

Putnam, Robert. 1996. "The Strange Disappearance of Civic America." *The American Prospect*, no. 24 (Winter): 34-48.

Richardson, J. David. 1995. "Income Inequality and Trade: How to Think and What to Conclude." *Journal of Economic Perspectives* 9, no. 3 (Summer): 33-55.

Richardson, J. David, and Elena B. Khripounova. 1996. "Estimating the 'Market-Power Component' of International Trade's Impact on U.S. Labor." Syracuse University. Photocopy.

Rodrik, Dani. 1994. "The Rush to Free Trade in the Developing World: Why So Late? Why Now? Will It Last?" In S. Haggard and S. B. Webb, *Voting for Reform: Democracy, Political Liberalization, and Economic Adjustment.* New York: Oxford University Press.

Rodrik, Dani. 1995. "Developing Countries after the Uruguay Round." In UN Conference on Trade and Development, *International and Monetary Issues for the 1990s*, vol. 6. New York: United Nations.

Rodrik, Dani. 1996. *Why Do More Open Economies Have Bigger Governments?* NBER Working Paper No. 5537. Cambridge, MA: National Bureau of Economic Research.

Rodrik, Dani. N.d. "Labor Standards in International Trade: Do They Matter and What Do We Do About Them?" In Robert Lawrence, Dani Rodrik, and John Whalley, *Emerging Agenda in Global Trade: High Stakes for Developing Countries.* Washington: Overseas Development Council. Forthcoming.

Ruggie, John G. 1994. "Trade, Protectionism, and the Future of Welfare Capitalism." *Journal of International Affairs* 48, no. 1 (Summer): 1-11.

Ruggie, John G. 1995. "At Home Abroad, Abroad at Home: International Liberalization and Domestic Stability in the New World Economy." *Millennium: Journal of International Studies* 24, no. 3: 507-26.

Sachs, Jeffrey, and Howard Shatz. 1994. "Trade and Jobs in U.S. Manufacturing." *Brookings Papers on Economic Activity* 1: 1-84. Washington: Brookings Institution.

Sachs, Jeffrey, and Andrew Warner. 1995. "Economic Reform and the Process of Global Integration." *Brookings Papers on Economic Activity* 1: 1-95. Washington: Brookings Institution.

Sandel, Michael J. 1996. *Democracy's Discontent: America in Search of a Public Philosophy.* Cambridge, MA: Harvard University Press.

Sapir, Andre. 1996. "*Trade Liberalization and the Harmonization of Social Policies: Lessons from European Integration.*" In Jagdish N. Bhagwati and Robert E. Hudec, *Fair Trade and Harmonization: Prerequisites for Free Trade?, vol. 1: Economic Analysis.* Cambridge, MA: MIT Press.

Saxonhouse, Gary. 1993. "What Does Japanese Trade Structure Tell Us About Japanese Trade Policy?" *Journal of Economic Perspectives* 7, no. 3 (Summer): 21-43.

Schiff, Maurice. 1992. "Social Capital, Labor Mobility, and Welfare." *Rationality and Society* 4, no. 2 (April): 157-75.

Schott, Jeffrey J. 1990. *The Global Trade Negotiations: What Can Be Achieved?* POLICY ANALYSES IN INTERNATIONAL ECONOMICS 29. Washington: Institute for International Economics.

Sinn, Hans-Werner. 1995. "A Theory of the Welfare State." *Scandinavian Journal of Economics* 97, no. 4: 495-526.

Sinn, Hans-Werner. 1996. "Social Insurance, Incentives, and Risk Taking." *International Tax and Public Finance* 3: 259-80.

Slaughter, Matthew. 1996. "International Trade and Labor-Demand Elasticities." Dartmouth College. Unpublished paper.

Srinivasan, T. N. 1995. "International Trade and Labour Standards." Yale University. Unpublished paper.

Tanzi, Vito, and Ludger Schuknecht. 1995. *The Growth of Government and the Reform of the State in Industrial Countries.* IMF Working Paper WP/95/130. Washington: International Monetary Fund.

Taylor-Gooby, Peter. 1985. *Public Opinion, Ideology, and the Welfare State.* London: Routledge & Kegan Paul.

Taylor-Gooby, Peter. 1989. "The Role of the State." In R. Jowell, S. Witherspoon, and Lindsay Brook, *British Social Attitudes: Special International Report*, vol. 6. Aldershot: Gower Publishing.

US Department of Labor. 1994. *International Labor Standards and Global Economic Integration: Proceedings of a Symposium.* Washington: Bureau of International Labor Affairs.

Vernon, Raymond. N.d. "In the Hurricane's Eye: Multinational Enterprises in the Next Century." Harvard University. Unpublished manuscript.

Wallerstein, Michael, and Adam Przeworski. 1995. "Capital Taxation with Open Borders." *Review of International Political Economy* 2, no. 3 (Summer): 425-45.

Walzer, Michael. 1983. *Spheres of Justice: A Defense of Pluralism and Equality.* New York: Basic Books.

Williamson, Jeffrey. 1996. *Globalization and Inequality Then and Now: The Late 19th and Late 20th Centuries Compared.* NBER Working Paper No. 5491. Cambridge, MA: National Bureau of Economic Research.

Wood, Adrian. 1994. *North-South Trade, Employment, and Inequality: Changing Fortunes in a Skill-Driven World.* Oxford, England: Clarendon Press.

Wood, Adrian. 1995. "How Trade Hurt Unskilled Workers." *Journal of Economic Perspectives* 9, no. 3 (Summer): 57-80.

Index

AFL-CIO, 76
Agreement on Safeguards (WTO), 83
Alesina, Alberto, 45, 70n, 95
Antidumping proceedings, 37, 78, 78n,
    79–84
Asea, Patrick, 63, 98
Australia, social spending in, 50t, 61
    public support for, 66, 66t
Austria, social spending in, 50t, 50–51, 61
    public support for, 66, 66t

Bagwell, Kyle, 82n, 95
Bairoch, Paul, 7, 95
Bargaining, labor, 23, 36, 39, 74–75
Barro, Robert J., 94, 95
Belgium, 50t, 52, 82
Bergsten, C. Fred, 47, 78n, 95
Berman, Eli, 16n, 16, 95
Bhagwati, Jagdish N., 3n, 14, 22, 23n, 95
Blanchflower, David G., 24, 95
Blocked exchanges, 35–36
Blondel, Marc, 44
BMW, 44
Boeing, 74
Borjas, George, 13–15, 23n, 24, 96
Bound, John, 16n, 95

Bovard, James, 32, 37, 96
Bressand, Albert, 82n, 97
Buchanan, Patrick, 1n, 3, 69

Cameron, David, 51, 96
Canada
    free trade agreement with U.S., 41n
    social spending in, 50t, 52, 61
Capital, taxes on, 54–55, 63
Capitalism, global, 74
Capital mobility, 6, 8, 73
    and demand for labor, 54–55, 57, 61,
        87–93
Castañeda, Jorge, 70–71, 96
Cato Institute, 32
Cayman Islands, 82
CEA. See Council of Economic Advisers
Child labor, 29–35, 45–46
Child Labor Deterrence Act, 32n, 33
China, 13, 74–75, 83n
Chirac, Jacques, 41
Cline, William R., 3n, 13, 15, 96
Collective bargaining, 35, 39
Collins, Susan, 3n, 96
Commission of the European
    Communities, 39, 96

Page numbers followed by *t*, *f*, and *n* indicate tables, figures, and footnotes, respectively, and page numbers in italics indicate complete reference listings for the cited author or work.

Commodity prices, 8
Communitarian movement, 2
Community spirit, 70, 70n
Comparative advantage, 3
  effects of globalization on, 23, 30, 34
  and labor standards, 45–46, 75
  and social dumping, 39
  and specialization, 55
Competition, unfair, 40, 79–80
Competitive advantage, 23
Competitiveness, as excuse for domestic
    reform, 79–80
Consumption risk, 55–57, 56t
Convergence, 37, 40–41, 48
Costs, nonwage, incidence of, 17–19
Council of Economic Advisers, 22n, 96
Crick, Bernard R., 70, 96
Currency devaluation, 19

Davis, Donald R., 96
Dehejia, Vivek H., 23n, 95
Denmark, 6, 41n, 41, 61
"Desperate" exchanges, 35
Developing countries
  effects of globalization on, 70–71
  social insurance in, 59–60
Dixit, Avinash, 17n, 73n, 76n, 96
Donahue, Thomas R., 16
Downsizing, 22
Durable goods industries, 15

Easterly, William, 70n, 96
Eastern Europe, 1
ECJ. See European Court of Justice
Economists
  approach to globalization, 3
  role of, 72–74
EEC. See European Economic
    Community
Employment, instability of, 21–23
Employment relationship, 4–5, 23–25
  consequences of trade for, 11–27
Enterprise surplus, redistribution of, 25
Environmental policy, costs of, 46
Equal pay, 38–39
Escape clause mechanisms, 73, 78, 78n,
    80–82, 82n
Esping-Andersen, Gösta, 49, 96
Etzioni, Amitai, 2, 96
European Commission, 39
European Court of Justice, 40
European Economic Community, 38. See
    also specific countries
  antidumping proceedings, 37, 78

integration and social policy in, 38–44,
    80
labor advocates in, 75–76
labor market in, 11–12, 25
ratio of exports to national income, 7,
    7f
Social Charter, 39–40, 44
social dumping in, 39n, 44
social spending in, 49, 50t
  public support for, 66
trade policy in, 78–83, 81n
External risk
  estimate of, time-varying, 61n
  exposure to, 53–55
    versus openness, 58
  importance of, 55–57, 56t
    cross-country evidence on, 57–60,
      59t

Factor endowments model, 13–14, 16, 47
Fair labor standards, 33n, 36
Fair trade, demands for, 5, 31–38, 77,
    80–81
Farber, Henry S., 21–23, 96
Financial Times, 81n, 82
Finland, 61
Foreign Corrupt Practices Act (FCPA) of
    1977, 47, 81, 81n
Foreign direct investment (FDI), 12
Foreign investment, tax evasion via,
    81–82
France, 38
  labor strikes in, 1, 41–44, 80
  social spending in, 49–51, 50t, 51f, 61
  tax rates in, 63–64, 65f
Freeman, Richard, 11, 13–14, 19, 25, 76n,
    96
Free trade
  defense of, 31, 48
  social legitimacy and, 65, 72, 76–77
Friedman, Thomas L., 1n, 96

Garrett, Geoffrey, 51, 96
General Agreement on Tariffs and Trade
    (GATT), 5, 32n–33n, 83
Germany, 1, 37
  social spending in, 49–51, 51f, 61
  public support for, 66, 66t
Global Awareness Society International,
    2n
Globalization. See also Trade
  backlash against, 1n, 1–4, 69
  economists' approach to, 3, 72–74
  historical aspects of, 7–9

measures of, 7–8
popular misconceptions about, 74–75
tensions generated by, 3–7, 29–48, 73
Goldsmith, Sir James, 2–3
Gold standard, 7–8
Goods, low-skill-intensive, relative price
of, 14, 27
Gottschalk, Peter, 21–22, *96*
Government
role of, 77–80
social spending by. *See* Social
insurance
Government consumption, 58, 61
Greider, William, 74–75
Group of Seven, Lyon summit, 2–3

Health and safety regulations, 35, 39–40
Heckscher-Ohlin-Samuelson factor
endowments model, 13–14, 16, 47
Hines, James, 47, *97*
Hirschman, Albert O., 70, 85, *97*
Hoekman, Bernard M., 82, *97*
Hoover Europe, 44
Howell, David, 24, *97*
Hudec, Robert E., *95*
Hufbauer, Gary C., 83n, *97*
Humanitarian goals, and trade policy
formulation, 33–35

Immigration, 8, 14, 26–27
Import tariffs, 72n
Income redistribution, 30–31
Income risk, 55–57, 56t
Income transfers, 49, 51f, 55, 59, 61, 79
Industrial policy, 46–47
Input-output coefficients, 31n
Insider trading ban, 31n
Internal risk, 57
International conflicts, economic sources
of, 5–6, 72n
International institutions, role of, 81–85
International Monetary Fund, 62n
International Trade Organization, 33n
Ireland, 41n, 50t, 82
Irwin, Douglas A., 8, *97*
Italy, 40
social spending in, 50t, 61
public support for, 66, 66t
Ito, Takatoshi, 82n, *97*

Jaffee, Adam B., 46, *97*
Japan, 1, 37, 46–47
openness to trade, 58

ratio of exports to national income, 7,
7f
social spending in, 49–51, 50t, 51f, 52,
61
as target of unilateral trade policy, 80,
81n
Job loss, rate of, 21–23, 25
definition of, 21n
Juppé, Alain, 42–43

Kapstein, Ethan, 2, *97*
Katz, Lawrence F., 13–14, 24, *96–97*
Katzenstein, Peter J., 50–51, *97*
Keefer, Philip, 70n, *97*
Keiretsu, 47
Keynes, John Maynard, 48n, 72n, 72, *97*
Khripounova, Elena B., 16–17, 23n, 27, *98*
Knack, Stephen, 70n, *97*
Kodak-Fuji dispute, 37–38
Korea, South, 1–2
Kostecki, Michael M., 82, *97*
Kozul-Wright, Richard, 7, *95*
Krueger, Alan, 33, 33n–34n, *97*
Krugman, Paul, 3n, 13–14, 79n, *97*

Labor. *See also* Employment; Wages
bargaining power of, 23, 36, 39, 75–76
child, 29–35, 45–46
demand for, 16–27, 87–93
shocks to, 19–20, 20f
immigrant, 8, 14, 26–27
mobility of, 8, 40, 73, 77
prison, 32, 48
rent sharing by, 15, 24–25
skill mix of, 76n
slave, 48, 84
substitutability of, 4, 17, 22–27
taxes on, 18–19, 45, 54–55, 63
unskilled, 4, 11–17, 23, 75
demand for, 25–27
Labor advocates, role of, 75–77
Labor costs, 75–76
Labor demand curve, 20, 20f
Labor laws, 34–36, 39
Labor market, 11–27
deinstitutionalization of, 23–25
instability of, 19–23
postdisplacement outcomes in, 22–23
Labor-market insurance, 79
Labor productivity, 74–76
Labor standards
costs of, distribution of, 17–18, 18f
effects of labor costs on, 45–46
effects of trade flows on, 46

and formulation of trade policy, 33–35, 39, 45, 77
Labor strikes, French, 1, 41–44, 80
Labor supply curve, 18, 18f
Labor unions
  backlash from, 2
  efficiency costs of, 25n–26n
  and French strike, 42–44
  political power of, 75–76
  weakening of, 23–25
Latin America, 2
Lawrence, Robert Z., 13–15, 47, 82n, 97
Leamer, Edward, 13, 17n, 97
Le Chatelier-Samuelson principle, 17n
Lee, Jong-Wha, 94, 95
Leebron, David W., 76, 97
Legitimacy issues, 31–35, 65, 71, 80–81, 83
Leibfried, Stephan, 39–40, 40n, 98
Levine, Ross, 70n, 96
Levy, Frank, 11n, 98
Liberalism, embedded, 65–66, 72, 77
Libertarians, 32
Lindert, Peter H., 49n, 98
Lochner v. New York, 35–36
Londregan, John, 76n, 96
Luxembourg, 52

Maastricht criteria, 1, 41–44, 80
Machin, Stephen, 16n, 95
Maguire, Matthew, 42n
Major, John, 39
Marketization, 85
Marxian socialism, 72
Mayer, William G., 66n, 98
Medicare, 66
Mendoza, Enrique G., 63, 98
Mexico, 32n–33n, 70–71
Migrant workers, 34
Milesi-Ferretti, Gian Maria, 61n, 63, 98
Minimum wage laws, 35–36
Mishel, Lawrence, 98
Mitchell, Daniel J. B., 24, 98
Mitchell, Deborah, 51, 96
Moffitt, Robert, 21–22, 96
Multilateral trade policies, 5, 48, 73, 77–82, 82n
Multinational corporations, 2n, 16, 44, 80–81
Murdoch, Rupert, 16

NAFTA. See North American Free Trade Agreement

National practices, differences in
  effects on trade, 5–6, 32–33, 37, 44–48, 80–81
  harmonization of, 73, 79–80
National sovereignty, 36n–37n, 40
Netherlands, 6, 82
  social spending in, 49, 50t, 50–52, 61
New York Times, 37, 42–44
New Zealand, 50t, 58
Noland, Marcus, 47, 95, 98
North American Free Trade Agreement, 2, 33n–34n
Norway, 50t, 61
Nozick, Robert, 31n, 98
Nye, Joseph, 67, 98

Occupational health and safety regulations, 35, 39–40
OECD. See Organization for Economic Cooperation and Development
Old-age insurance, 58, 66, 79
One World, Ready or Not: The Manic Logic of Global Capitalism (Greider), 74–75
Openness
  effects on labor market, 19–20, 20f
  versus exposure to external risk, 58
  measurement of, 58
  relationship between taxes and, 63–65, 64t, 65f
  and social insurance, 51–55, 52f–53f
    balance between, 76–77
    cross-country evidence on, 57–60, 59t
    in OECD countries, 60–64, 62t
Organization for Economic Cooperation and Development, 45, 47n, 49, 79n, 81, 81n. See also specific countries
  countries in, government spending by, 60–64, 62t
Oswald, Andrew J., 24, 95
Outsourcing, 4, 12, 30, 32–34, 46, 70
  definition of, 4n

Paid holiday schemes, 38
Penn World Tables, 58, 94, 98
Perez-Lopez, Jorge F., 83n, 98
Perot, Ross, 2
Perotti, Roberto, 41, 45, 51, 61n, 95, 98
Peterson, Steven R., 46, 97
Pierson, Paul, 39–40, 40n, 98
Polanyi, Karl, 71
Political backlash, against trade, 1, 3, 69
Political power, of labor unions, 75–76
Pollution abatements, costs of, 46

Portney, Paul R., 46, *97*
Portugal, 39
Prison labor, 32, 48
Production function, 31*n*
Production labor, demand for, 17
Product markets, volatility in, 23
Protectionism, 1, 3, 6, 9, 33–34, 38, 48, 53, 69, 72, 75–76, 85
Protocol on Social Policy (Maastricht treaty), 41
Przeworski, Adam, 54*n*, *99*
The Public Interest, 66*n*
Public opinion
  importance of, 84, 84*n*
  on social spending, 65–66, 66*t*, 66*n*
Putnam, Robert, 70*n*, *98*

Ramey, Valerie, 15, 23*n*, 24, *96*
Razin, A., 63, *98*
Rent sharing, 15, 24–25
Republican party, 1, 69
Research and development activities, 31–32
Retaliation, 81
Richardson, J. David, 13, 16–17, 23*n*, 27, *98*
Rodrik, Dani, 30*n*, 45, 52–53, 60*n*, 60, 70*n*, 83*n*, *95*, *98*
Roosevelt, Franklin D., 36
Rose, Andy, 62*n*
Rosen, Howard F., 83*n*, *97*
Ruggie, John G., 36, 65, 67, 71, *98*
Russia, 1

Sachs, Jeffrey, 13, *99*
Safeguard measures, 83–85
Samuelson, Paul, 3
Sandel, Michael J., 2, 36, *99*
Sanfey, Peter, 24, *95*
San Francisco Chronicle, 44
Sapir, Andre, 38, 38*n*–39*n*, 39–40, 44, *99*
Saxonhouse, Gary, 47, *99*
Schiff, Maurice, *99*
Schott, Jeffrey J., 78*n*, *99*
Schuknecht, Ludger, 50, 79, *99*
Scotland, 44
Serious injury, 83, 83*n*
Shatz, Howard, 13, *99*
Single European Act, 39
Sinn, Hans-Werner, 65*n*, *99*
Skill premium. *See* Wage inequality
Slaughter, Matthew, 13–14, 17, 27, *97*, *99*
Slave labor, 48, 84

Social Charter (European Community), 39–40, 44
Social dumping, 39*n*, 44
Social insurance, 49–67
  in Europe, 38–44
  importance of, 53, 78–79
  increases in, 49, 51*f*
  in lower-income countries, 59–60
  measurement of, 58
  in OECD countries, 60–64, 62*t*
  public support for, 65–66, 66*t*
  tax burden of, 63–65, 64*t*, 65*f*
  and trade openness, 6, 9, 45–47, 51–55, 52*f*–53*f*
    balance between, 76–77
    cross-country evidence on, 57–60, 59*t*
    and external risk exposure, 55–57
    role of economists in, 72–74
Socialism, 72
Social security, 58, 66, 79
Social stability, tensions between globalization and, 7, 29–48, 69–71, 73
  sources of, 4–7
Spain, 39, 50*t*
Specialization, 55
Srinivasan, T. N., 33, 35, *99*
Staiger, Robert W., 82*n*, *95*
Stavins, Robert, 46, *97*
Summers, Lawrence H., 24, *97*
Supreme Court, 35–36
Sweden, 6
  social spending in, 49, 50*t*, 50–51, 61
Switzerland, 50*t*, 51

Tanzi, Vito, 50, 79, *99*
Taxation
  capital, 54–55, 63
  European policy on, 40
  evasion of, via foreign investment, 81–82
  at global level, 73, 81
  labor, 18–19, 45, 54–55, 63
  relationship between openness and, 63–65, 64*t*, 65*f*
  and social insurance burden, 63–65, 64*t*, 65*f*
  unitary, 54*n*
Taylor-Gooby, Peter, 66, *99*
Technological change, skill-biased, 12, 15–16, 24–25, 31, 48, 71
Terms-of-trade improvement, 31*n*
Terms-of-trade volatility, 54, 59, 61–63

Tesar, L., 63, *98*
Tobin tax, 73
Trade. *See also* Globalization
  distributional consequences of, 30–31
  exposure to, and country size, 60*n*
  fair, demands for, 5, 31–38, 77, 80–81
  free
    defense of, 31, 48
    social legitimacy and, 65, 72, 76–77
  gains from, 30*n*, 30–31, 76
  new issues in, 36–38
  openness to. *See* Openness
  self-sufficiency in, 48*n*
Trade barriers, 32, 48, 69, 72, 77, 78*n*
Trade flows, effects on labor standards, 46
Trade policy
  formulation of
    in global economy, 71–72
    and labor standard concerns, 33–35, 39, 45
    role of economists in, 72–74
  multilateral, 5, 48, 73, 77–82, 82*n*
  in response to globalization tensions, 3, 73
Trade practices, corrupt, 47, 80–81
Trades of last resort, 35
Trade volumes, 7, 27
Treaty of Rome, 38–39
Turkey, 1*n*, 52

Unemployment, 21–23, 25, 79
Unemployment insurance, 66
United Kingdom, 8
  and EEC social policy disputes, 39, 41, 44
  openness to trade, 58
  social spending in, 49–51, 50*t*, 51*f*, 61
    public support for, 66, 66*t*
  tax rates in, 63–64, 65*f*
United States
  antidumping proceedings, 37, 78, 78*n*
  environmental policy in, 46
  escape clause action in, 78*n*
  free trade agreement with Canada, 41
  government growth in, 49–52, 50*t*, 51*f*
  immigration to, 8, 14
  labor advocates in, 75–76
  labor laws, 35–36
  labor market in, 11–12, 27
    instability of, 21*t*, 21–23

  leadership role of, 71
  openness to trade, 58
  ratio of exports to national income, 7, 7*f*
  social spending in, 61
    public support for, 66, 66*t*
  tax rates in, 64, 65*f*
  trade deficit, 77
  trade policy in, 78–83, 81*n*
Uruguay Round, 82
U.S. Commerce Department, 78*n*
U.S. Department of Labor, 16, 45, *99*
U.S. Trade Representative, 80

Vernon, Raymond, 2, *99*
Voluntary export restraints (VERs), 82

Wade, Robert, 1*n*
Wage cuts, 19
Wage inequality, 11, 13–16, 20–21, 23–25
Wages
  determination of, 24–25
  effects of international trade on, 3–5, 13–14, 75–76
  instability of, 21, 21*t*
  minimum, 35–36
Wagner's law, 61
Wallerstein, Michael, 54*n*, *99*
Walzer, Michael, 35, *99*
Warner, Andrew, *99*
Watergate scandal, 47
Welfare spending, 58, 66. *See also* Social insurance
West Coast Hotel Co. v. Parrish, 36
Williamson, Jeffrey, 8, *99*
Women, labor standards for, 36, 38–39
Wood, Adrian, 13–14, *99*
Workers. *See* Labor
Working conditions. *See* Labor standards
World Bank, 94
World Trade Organization (WTO), 2–3, 5, 32, 37
  Agreement on Safeguards (WTO), 83
  congressional votes over, 33*n*–34*n*
  escape clause mechanisms, 73, 78, 78*n*, 80–82, 82*n*
  monitoring role for, 84

Xian Aircraft Company, 74–75

Zyuganov, Gennady, 1

Other Publications from the Institute for International Economics

POLICY ANALYSES IN INTERNATIONAL ECONOMICS Series

1 **The Lending Policies of the International Monetary Fund**
John Williamson/*August 1982*
ISBN paper 0-88132-000-5   72 pp.

2 **"Reciprocity": A New Approach to World Trade Policy?**
William R. Cline/*September 1982*
ISBN paper 0-88132-001-3   41 pp.

3 **Trade Policy in the 1980s**
C. Fred Bergsten and William R. Cline/*November 1982*
(out of print)   ISBN paper 0-88132-002-1   84 pp.
Partially reproduced in the book *Trade Policy in the 1980s.*

4 **International Debt and the Stability of the World Economy**
William R. Cline/*September 1983*
ISBN paper 0-88132-010-2   134 pp.

5 **The Exchange Rate System,** Second Edition
John Williamson/*September 1983, rev. June 1985*
(out of print)   ISBN paper 0-88132-034-X   61 pp.

6 **Economic Sanctions in Support of Foreign Policy Goals**
Gary Clyde Hufbauer and Jeffrey J. Schott/*October 1983*
ISBN paper 0-88132-014-5   109 pp.

7 **A New SDR Allocation?**
John Williamson/*March 1984*
ISBN paper 0-88132-028-5   61 pp.

8 **An International Standard for Monetary Stabilization**
Ronald I. McKinnon/*March 1984*
(out of print)   ISBN paper 0-88132-018-8   108 pp.

9 **The Yen/Dollar Agreement: Liberalizing Japanese Capital Markets**
Jeffrey A. Frankel/*December 1984*
ISBN paper 0-88132-035-8   86 pp.

10 **Bank Lending to Developing Countries: The Policy Alternatives**
C. Fred Bergsten, William R. Cline, and John Williamson/*April 1985*
ISBN paper 0-88132-032-3   221 pp.

11 **Trading for Growth: The Next Round of Trade Negotiations**
Gary Clyde Hufbauer and Jeffrey J. Schott/*September 1985*
(out of print)   ISBN paper 0-88132-033-1   109 pp.

12 **Financial Intermediation Beyond the Debt Crisis**
Donald R. Lessard and John Williamson/*September 1985*
(out of print)   ISBN paper 0-88132-021-8   130 pp.

13 **The United States-Japan Economic Problem**
C. Fred Bergsten and William R. Cline/*October 1985, 2d ed. January 1987*
(out of print)   ISBN paper 0-88132-060-9   180 pp.

14 **Deficits and the Dollar: The World Economy at Risk**
Stephen Marris/*December 1985, 2d ed. November 1987*
(out of print)   ISBN paper 0-88132-067-6   415 pp.

15 **Trade Policy for Troubled Industries**
Gary Clyde Hufbauer and Howard F. Rosen/*March 1986.*
ISBN paper 0-88132-020-X   111 pp.

16 The United States and Canada: The Quest for Free Trade
Paul Wonnacott, with an Appendix by John Williamson/*March 1987*
ISBN paper 0-88132-056-0   188 pp.

17 Adjusting to Success: Balance of Payments Policy
in the East Asian NICs
Bela Balassa and John Williamson/*June 1987, rev. April 1990*
ISBN paper 0-88132-101-X   160 pp.

18 Mobilizing Bank Lending to Debtor Countries
William R. Cline/*June 1987*
ISBN paper 0-88132-062-5   100 pp.

19 Auction Quotas and United States Trade Policy
C. Fred Bergsten, Kimberly Ann Elliott, Jeffrey J. Schott, and
Wendy E. Takacs/*September 1987*
ISBN paper 0-88132-050-1   254 pp.

20 Agriculture and the GATT: Rewriting the Rules
Dale E. Hathaway/*September 1987*
ISBN paper 0-88132-052-8   169 pp.

21 Anti-Protection: Changing Forces in United States Trade Politics
I. M. Destler and John S. Odell/*September 1987*
ISBN paper 0-88132-043-9   220 pp.

22 Targets and Indicators: A Blueprint for the International
Coordination of Economic Policy
John Williamson and Marcus H. Miller/*September 1987*
ISBN paper 0-88132-051-X   118 pp.

23 Capital Flight: The Problem and Policy Responses
Donald R. Lessard and John Williamson/*December 1987*
(out of print)   ISBN paper 0-88132-059-5   80 pp.

24 United States-Canada Free Trade: An Evaluation of the Agreement
Jeffrey J. Schott/*April 1988*
ISBN paper 0-88132-072-2   48 pp.

25 Voluntary Approaches to Debt Relief
John Williamson/*September 1988, rev. May 1989*
ISBN paper 0-88132-098-6   80 pp.

26 American Trade Adjustment: The Global Impact
William R. Cline/*March 1989*
ISBN paper 0-88132-095-1   98 pp.

27 More Free Trade Areas?
Jeffrey J. Schott/*May 1989*
ISBN paper 0-88132-085-4   88 pp.

28 The Progress of Policy Reform in Latin America
John Williamson/*January 1990*
ISBN paper 0-88132-100-1   106 pp.

29 The Global Trade Negotiations: What Can Be Achieved?
Jeffrey J. Schott/*September 1990*
ISBN paper 0-88132-137-0   72 pp.

30 Economic Policy Coordination: Requiem or Prologue?
Wendy Dobson/*April 1991*
ISBN paper 0-88132-102-8   162 pp.

31 The Economic Opening of Eastern Europe
John Williamson/*May 1991*   ISBN paper 0-88132-186-9   92 pp.

32 Eastern Europe and the Soviet Union in the World Economy
Susan M. Collins and Dani Rodrik/*May 1991*
ISBN paper 0-88132-157-5   152 pp.

33 African Economic Reform: The External Dimension
    Carol Lancaster/*June 1991*
                        ISBN paper 0-88132-096-X   82 pp.

34 Has the Adjustment Process Worked?
    Paul R. Krugman/*October 1991*
                        ISBN paper 0-88132-116-8   80 pp.

35 From Soviet disUnion to Eastern Economic Community?
    Oleh Havrylyshyn and John Williamson/*October 1991*
                        ISBN paper 0-88132-192-3   84 pp.

36 Global Warming: The Economic Stakes
    William R. Cline/*May 1992*
                        ISBN paper 0-88132-172-9   128 pp.

37 Trade and Payments After Soviet Disintegration
    John Williamson/*June 1992*
                        ISBN paper 0-88132-173-7   96 pp.

38 Trade and Migration: NAFTA and Agriculture
    Philip L. Martin/*October 1993*
                        ISBN paper 0-88132-201-6   160 pp.

39 The Exchange Rate System and the IMF: A Modest Agenda
    Morris Goldstein/*June 1995*
                        ISBN paper 0-88132-219-9   104 pp.

40 What Role for Currency Boards?
    John Williamson/*September 1995*
                        ISBN paper 0-88132-222-9   64 pp.

41 Predicting External Imbalances for the United States and Japan
    William R. Cline/*September 1995*
                        ISBN paper 0-88132-220-2   104 pp.

42 Standards and APEC: An Action Agenda
    John S. Wilson/*October 1995*
                        ISBN paper 0-88132-223-7   176 pp.

43 Fundamental Tax Reform and Border Tax Adjustments
    Gary Clyde Hufbauer assisted by Carol Gabyzon/*January 1996*
                        ISBN paper 0-88132-225-3   108 pp.

44 Global Telecom Talks: A Trillion Dollar Deal
    Ben A. Petrazzini/*June 1996*
                        ISBN paper 0-88132-230-X   128 pp.

45 WTO 2000: Setting the Course for World Trade
    Jeffrey J. Schott/*September 1996*
                        ISBN paper 0-88132-234-2   72 pp.

46 The National Economic Council: A Work in Progress
    I. M. Destler/*November 1996*
                        ISBN paper 0-88132-239-3   90 pp.

BOOKS

IMF Conditionality
John Williamson, editor/*1983*
                        ISBN cloth 0-88132-006-4   695 pp.

Trade Policy in the 1980s
William R. Cline, editor/*1983*
 (out of print)   ISBN paper 0-88132-031-5   810 pp.

Subsidies in International Trade
Gary Clyde Hufbauer and Joanna Shelton Erb/*1984*
                        ISBN cloth 0-88132-004-8   299 pp.

International Debt: Systemic Risk and Policy Response
William R. Cline/*1984*   ISBN cloth 0-88132-015-3   336 pp.

Trade Protection in the United States: 31 Case Studies
Gary Clyde Hufbauer, Diane E. Berliner, and Kimberly Ann Elliott/*1986*
 (out of print)   ISBN paper 0-88132-040-4   371 pp.

Toward Renewed Economic Growth in Latin America
Bela Balassa, Gerardo M. Bueno, Pedro-Pablo Kuczynski,
and Mario Henrique Simonsen/*1986*
(out of stock)   ISBN paper 0-88132-045-5   205 pp.

Capital Flight and Third World Debt
Donald R. Lessard and John Williamson, editors/*1987*
(out of print)   ISBN paper 0-88132-053-6   270 pp.

The Canada-United States Free Trade Agreement: The Global Impact
Jeffrey J. Schott and Murray G. Smith, editors/*1988*
                                   ISBN paper 0-88132-073-0   211 pp.

World Agricultural Trade: Building a Consensus
William M. Miner and Dale E. Hathaway, editors/*1988*
                                   ISBN paper 0-88132-071-3   226 pp.

Japan in the World Economy
Bela Balassa and Marcus Noland/*1988*
                                   ISBN paper 0-88132-041-2   306 pp.

America in the World Economy: A Strategy for the 1990s
C. Fred Bergsten/*1988*   ISBN cloth 0-88132-089-7   235 pp.
                                   ISBN paper 0-88132-082-X   235 pp.

Managing the Dollar: From the Plaza to the Louvre
Yoichi Funabashi/*1988, 2d ed. 1989*
                                   ISBN paper 0-88132-097-8   307 pp.

United States External Adjustment and the World Economy
William R. Cline/*May 1989*   ISBN paper 0-88132-048-X   392 pp.

Free Trade Areas and U.S. Trade Policy
Jeffrey J. Schott, editor/*May 1989*
                                   ISBN paper 0-88132-094-3   400 pp.

Dollar Politics: Exchange Rate Policymaking in the United States
I. M. Destler and C. Randall Henning/*September 1989*
(out of print)   ISBN paper 0-88132-079-X   192 pp.

Latin American Adjustment: How Much Has Happened?
John Williamson, editor/*April 1990*
                                   ISBN paper 0-88132-125-7   480 pp.

The Future of World Trade in Textiles and Apparel
William R. Cline/*1987, 2d ed. June 1990*
                                   ISBN paper 0-88132-110-9   344 pp.

**Completing the Uruguay Round: A Results-Oriented Approach
to the GATT Trade Negotiations**
Jeffrey J. Schott, editor/*September 1990*
                                   ISBN paper 0-88132-130-3   256 pp.

Economic Sanctions Reconsidered (in two volumes)
Economic Sanctions Reconsidered: Supplemental Case Histories
Gary Clyde Hufbauer, Jeffrey J. Schott, and Kimberly Ann Elliott/*1985, 2d ed. December 1990*
                                   ISBN cloth 0-88132-115-X   928 pp.
                                   ISBN paper 0-88132-105-2   928 pp.

Economic Sanctions Reconsidered: History and Current Policy
Gary Clyde Hufbauer, Jeffrey J. Schott, and Kimberly Ann Elliott/*December 1990*
                                   ISBN cloth 0-88132-136-2   288 pp.
                                   ISBN paper 0-88132-140-0   288 pp.
Pacific Basin Developing Countries: Prospects for the Future
Marcus Noland/*January 1991* ISBN   cloth 0-88132-141-9   250 pp.
(out of print)   ISBN paper 0-88132-081-1   250 pp.

Currency Convertibility in Eastern Europe
John Williamson, editor/*October 1991*
                                   ISBN paper 0-88132-128-1   396 pp.

International Adjustment and Financing: The Lessons of 1985-1991
C. Fred Bergsten, editor/*January 1992*
ISBN paper 0-88132-112-5   336 pp.

North American Free Trade: Issues and Recommendations
Gary Clyde Hufbauer and Jeffrey J. Schott/*April 1992*
ISBN paper 0-88132-120-6   392 pp.

Narrowing the U.S. Current Account Deficit
Allen J. Lenz/*June 1992*
(out of print)   ISBN paper 0-88132-103-6   640 pp.

The Economics of Global Warming
William R. Cline/*June 1992*   ISBN paper 0-88132-132-X   416 pp.

U.S. Taxation of International Income: Blueprint for Reform
Gary Clyde Hufbauer, assisted by Joanna M. van Rooij/*October 1992*
ISBN cloth 0-88132-178-8   304 pp.
ISBN paper 0-88132-134-6   304 pp.

Who's Bashing Whom? Trade Conflict in High-Technology Industries
Laura D'Andrea Tyson/*November 1992*
ISBN paper 0-88132-106-0   352 pp.

Korea in the World Economy
Il SaKong/*January 1993*   ISBN paper 0-88132-106-0   328 pp.

Pacific Dynamism and the International Economic System
C. Fred Bergsten and Marcus Noland, editors/*May 1993*
ISBN paper 0-88132-196-6   424 pp.

Economic Consequences of Soviet Disintegration
John Williamson, editor/*May 1993*
ISBN paper 0-88132-190-7   664 pp.

Reconcilable Differences? United States-Japan Economic Conflict
C. Fred Bergsten and Marcus Noland/*June 1993*
ISBN paper 0-88132-129-X   296 pp.

Does Foreign Exchange Intervention Work?
Kathryn M. Dominguez and Jeffrey A. Frankel/*September 1993*
ISBN paper 0-88132-104-4   192 pp.

Sizing Up U.S. Export Disincentives
J. David Richardson/*September 1993*
ISBN paper 0-88132-107-9   192 pp.

NAFTA: An Assessment
Gary Clyde Hufbauer and Jeffrey J. Schott/*rev. ed. October 1993*
ISBN paper 0-88132-199-0   216 pp.

Adjusting to Volatile Energy Prices
Philip K. Verleger, Jr./*November 1993*
ISBN paper 0-88132-069-2   288 pp.

The Political Economy of Policy Reform
John Williamson, editor/*January 1994*
ISBN paper 0-88132-195-8   624 pp.

Measuring the Costs of Protection in the United States
Gary Clyde Hufbauer and Kimberly Ann Elliott/*January 1994*
ISBN paper 0-88132-108-7   144 pp.

The Dynamics of Korean Economic Development
Cho Soon/*March 1994*   ISBN paper 0-88132-162-1   272 pp.

Reviving the European Union
C. Randall Henning, Eduard Hochreiter and Gary Clyde Hufbauer, editors/*April 1994*
ISBN paper 0-88132-208-3   192 pp.

China in the World Economy
Nicholas R. Lardy/*April 1994*
ISBN paper 0-88132-200-8   176 pp.

Greening the GATT: Trade, Environment, and the Future
Daniel C. Esty/ *July 1994*   ISBN paper 0-88132-205-9   344 pp.

Western Hemisphere Economic Integration
Gary Clyde Hufbauer and Jeffrey J. Schott/*July 1994*
                                    ISBN paper 0-88132-159-1   304 pp.

Currencies and Politics in the United States, Germany, and Japan
C. Randall Henning/*September 1994*
                                    ISBN paper 0-88132-127-3   432 pp.

Estimating Equilibrium Exchange Rates
John Williamson, editor/*September 1994*
                                    ISBN paper 0-88132-076-5   320 pp.

Managing the World Economy: Fifty Years After Bretton Woods
Peter B. Kenen, editor/*September 1994*
                                    ISBN paper 0-88132-212-1   448 pp.

Reciprocity and Retaliation in U.S. Trade Policy
Thomas O. Bayard and Kimberly Ann Elliott/*September 1994*
                                    ISBN paper 0-88132-084-6   528 pp.

The Uruguay Round: An Assessment
Jeffrey J. Schott, assisted by Johanna W. Buurman/*November 1994*
                                    ISBN paper 0-88132-206-7   240 pp.

Measuring the Costs of Protection in Japan
Yoko Sazanami, Shujiro Urata, and Hiroki Kawai/*January 1995*
                                    ISBN paper 0-88132-211-3   96 pp.

Foreign Direct Investment in the United States, Third Edition
Edward M. Graham and Paul R. Krugman/*January 1995*
                                    ISBN paper 0-88132-204-0   232 pp.

The Political Economy of Korea-United States Cooperation
C. Fred Bergsten and Il SaKong, editors/*February 1995*
                                    ISBN paper 0-88132-213-X   128 pp.

International Debt Reexamined
William R. Cline/*February 1995*

                                    ISBN paper 0-88132-083-8   560 pp.
American Trade Politics, Third Edition
I. M. Destler/*April 1995*   ISBN paper 0-88132-215-6   360 pp.
Managing Official Export Credits: The Quest for a Global Regime
John E. Ray/*July 1995*   ISBN paper 0-88132-207-5   344 pp.
Asia Pacific Fusion: Japan's Role in APEC
Yoichi Funabashi/*October 1995*
                                    ISBN paper 0-88132-224-5   312 pp.

Korea-United States Cooperation in the New World Order
C. Fred Bergsten and Il SaKong, editors/*February 1996*
                                    ISBN paper 0-88132-226-1   144 pp.

Why Exports Really Matter!   ISBN paper 0-88132-221-0   34 pp.
Why Exports Matter More!   ISBN paper 0-88132-229-6   36 pp.
J. David Richardson and Karin Rindal/*July 1995; February 1996*

Global Corporations and National Governments
Edward M. Graham/*May 1996*
                                    ISBN paper 0-88132-111-7   168 pp.

Global Economic Leadership and the Group of Seven
C. Fred Bergsten and C. Randall Henning/*May 1996*
                                    ISBN paper 0-88132-218-0   192 pp.

The Trading System After the Uruguay Round
John Whalley and Colleen Hamilton/*July 1996*
                                    ISBN paper 0-88132-131-1   224 pp.

Private Capital Flows to Emerging Markets After the Mexican Crisis
Guillermo A. Calvo, Morris Goldstein, and Eduard Hochreiter/*September 1996*
ISBN paper 0-88132-232-6   352 pp.

The Crawling Band as an Exchange Rate Regime:
Lessons from Chile, Colombia, and Israel
John Williamson/*September 1996*
ISBN paper 0-88132-231-8   192 pp.

Flying High: Civil Aviation in the Asia Pacific
Gary Clyde Hufbauer and Christopher Findlay/*November 1996*
ISBN paper 0-88132-231-8   232 pp.

Measuring the Costs of Visible Protection in Korea
Namdoo Kim/*November 1996*
ISBN paper 0-88132-236-9   112 pp.

The World Trading System: Challenges Ahead
Jeffrey J. Schott/*December 1996*
ISBN paper 0-88132-235-0   350 pp.

Has Globalization Gone Too Far?
Dani Rodrik/*March 1997*   ISBN cloth 0-88132-243-1   128 pp.
                             ISBN paper 0-88132-241-5   128 pp.

SPECIAL REPORTS
1   **Promoting World Recovery: A Statement on Global Economic Strategy**
    by Twenty-six Economists from Fourteen Countries/*December 1982*
    (out of print)   ISBN paper 0-88132-013-7   45 pp.
2   **Prospects for Adjustment in Argentina, Brazil, and Mexico:**
    Responding to the Debt Crisis   (out of print)
    John Williamson, editor/*June 1983*   ISBN paper 0-88132-016-1   71 pp.
3   **Inflation and Indexation: Argentina, Brazil, and Israel**
    John Williamson, editor/*March 1985*   ISBN paper 0-88132-037-4   191 pp.
4   **Global Economic Imbalances**
    C. Fred Bergsten, editor/*March 1986*   ISBN cloth 0-88132-038-2   126 pp.
                                             ISBN paper 0-88132-042-0   126 pp.
5   **African Debt and Financing**
    Carol Lancaster and John Williamson, editors/*May 1986*
    (out of print)   ISBN paper 0-88132-044-7   229 pp.
6   **Resolving the Global Economic Crisis: After Wall Street**
    Thirty-three Economists from Thirteen Countries/*December 1987*
                                 ISBN paper 0-88132-070-6   30 pp.
7   **World Economic Problems**
    Kimberly Ann Elliott and John Williamson, editors/*April 1988*
                                 ISBN paper 0-88132-055-2   298 pp.
    Reforming World Agricultural Trade
    Twenty-nine Professionals from Seventeen Countries/*1988*
                                 ISBN paper 0-88132-088-9   42 pp.
8   **Economic Relations Between the United States and Korea:**
    Conflict or Cooperation?
    Thomas O. Bayard and Soo-Gil Young, editors/*January 1989*
                                 ISBN paper 0-88132-068-4   192 pp.

WORKS IN PROGRESS

Liberalizing Financial Services
Michael Aho and Pierre Jacquet

The US-Korea Economic Relationship
C. Fred Bergsten and Il SaKong, editors

Trade, Jobs, and Income Distribution
William R. Cline

China's Entry to the World Economy
Richard N. Cooper

Corruption and the Global Economy
Kimberly Ann Elliott

Economic Sanctions After the Cold War
Kimberly Ann Elliott, Gary C. Hufbauer and Jeffrey J. Schott

Trade and Labor Standards
Kimberly Ann Elliott and Richard Freeman

Summitry of the Americas: A Progress Report
Richard Feinberg

Regional Trading Blocs in the World Economic System
Jeffrey A. Frankel

The New Transatlantic Marketplace:
Ellen Frost

The Case for An International Banking Standard
Morris Goldstein

Forecasting Financial Crises: Early Warning Signs for Emerging Markets
Morris Goldstein and Carmen Reinhart

Overseeing Global Capital Markets
Morris Goldstein and Peter Garber

Global Competition Policy
Edward M. Graham and J. David Richardson

Global Impact of Monetary Union in Europe
C. Randall Henning

Prospects for Western Hemisphere Free Trade
Gary Clyde Hufbauer and Jeffrey J. Schott

The Future of U.S. Foreign Aid
Carol Lancaster

The Economics of Korean Unification
Marcus Noland

The Case for Trade: A Modern Reconsideration
J. David Richardson

Who's Bashing Whom? Trade Conflict in High-Technology Industries, Second Edition
Laura D'Andrea Tyson

Visit our website at: http:/ / www.iie.com
E-mail address: orders@iie.com